# MORE Ghosts of Block Island

*by*

***Fran Migliaccio***

***Photography by Marea Mott***

***Art and photography by Gillian Stevens***

**Copyright © 2009 by Frances Huggard Migliaccio**
ISBN 978-0-9773639-1-9

ALL RIGHTS RESERVED.
No part of this book may be used or reproduced in any manner whatsoever without express written consent of the author.

Published by:
Frances Huggard Migliaccio
P.O. Box 412
Block Island, RI 02807
www.blockislandghosts.com

***To Rally,***

***of course,***

***for staying the course***

***and helping to see this through***

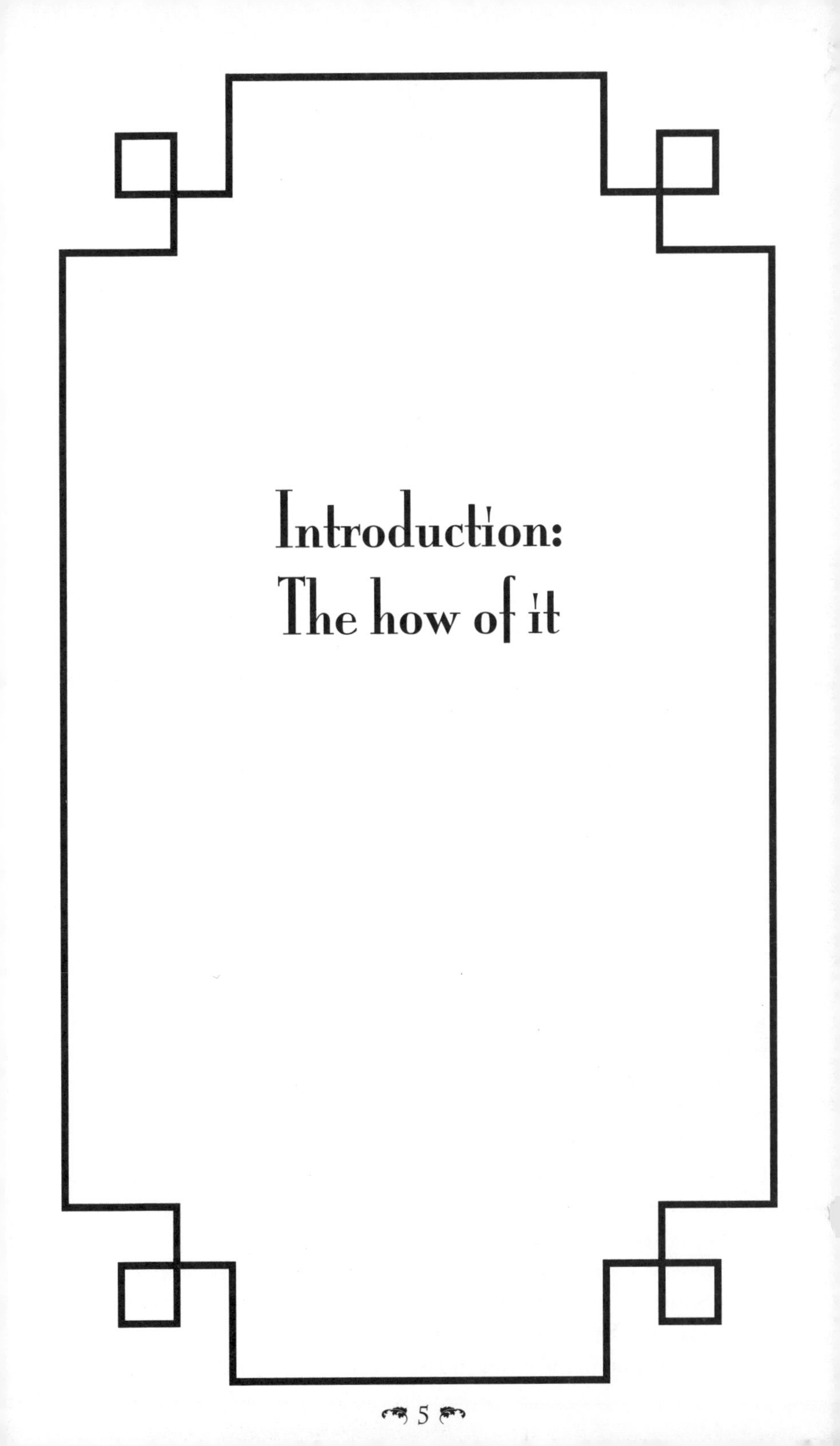

# Introduction: The how of it

GHOST STORIES ENGENDER MORE GHOST STORIES. When I began writing this book, three years after my first collection, *Ghosts of Block Island*, was published, I had a big fat file of notes, anecdotes, names and numbers of people in various places who had stories of ghosts on offer.

In putting together the stories for this book, I set out to find ghosts in new places on Block Island. In a couple of instances, I revisited former haunts, when unexpected and strong new stories or new facts about old places became apparent. With those few exceptions, the haunted locations written about in this book are new ones, to me if not to the ghosts.

I also wanted to hear from new and different storytellers, and was able to tap into the experiences of many new seers. I am grateful to every one of those people for sharing their stories with such generosity of time and spirit.

Writing this book was difficult at times. Ghosts, of course, have been attended by death, and deaths can be hard: hard to learn about, hard to ask about, hard on the memories of survivors, hard to write about. Some events that I uncovered in writing this book cut close to the bone. They affected people I hold dear, and brought great sadness to me as I learned of them. People who helped by telling me the truth behind the stories knew my purpose, and all were most gracious in sharing their knowledge and experiences.

There are those, of course, who persistently disbelieve in ghosts. Some, in fact, are people who admit to hearing or otherwise experiencing ghosts, as some of the stories in this book illustrate.

Non-believers are prone to dismiss ghost stories as having an ulterior purpose:

"Of course, they're all true!" said Merrill Slate jokingly in December 2005, after inquiring how my first book of ghost stories was doing. "Ghost stories were all made up to scare children so they wouldn't misbehave! But there's always an explanation.

"There was a man who used to steal potatoes from Summit Farm, when Shorty Littlefield lived up there. Shorty wondered why his potatoes just seemed to disappear. The man used to come the back way, walking over the hill from his house on Mitchell Lane. Shorty caught him, though. He knew his potatoes weren't disappearing into thin air!"

Others believe that ghost stories evolve as a sort of folklore, built on chance remarks or quips that take on the trappings of fact after repetition. Arthur Rose told me an anecdote that could have become the kernel of that kind of "ghost story":

"You know that driveway up into the cemetery?" Arthur asked me a few years ago. "Hiram Ball's house used to be at the corner where the wall goes up. He had a big orchard behind his place.

"Clarence Mitchell lived up there, near where John Tripler lives now. People used to call Clarence "Tadpole," and he got madder than the devil at the name!

"One day, Clarence was walking toward Dead-Eye's and he heard some kids counting stolen apples from the orchard: 'One for you, one for me…'

"Clarence took a fright, and ran to Dead-Eye's!

"'What's the matter, Tad?' he was asked.

"'I went by Hi Ball's place,' he told them, 'and the Lord and the Devil are countin' out the dead!'"

These stories are amusing, and I always enjoy hearing them.

Ghost stories, however, are something quite different: they involve the supernatural, and contain events that cannot be "explained away" by rational means. Ghost stories are mystery. They may be dark, or not so dark. They may be instructive. They may be amusing, even joyful. While ghost stories may entertain, they do not exist solely for that purpose.

Ghost stories tell of events which, when they occurred, may have made the storyteller's hair stand straight up on end. Or, the events might have given the storyteller a measure of comfort or peace, if the ghosts were there to reassure, or were the protective sorts who came to be like old friends to the humans around them.

Ghost stories leave in their wake seers and storytellers who know — beyond any shadow of doubt — that they have experienced something otherworldly, something supernatural, something: ghostly — for lack of a better word.

The people who shared these ghost stories with me are those people, those who know.

# A Word About Tours

PEOPLE HAVE OFTEN ASKED ME IF I OFFER GHOST TOURS. Because of that seeming interest, I once toyed with the idea and even put a line on my website, www.blockislandghosts.com, saying that small tours could be arranged. After initial inquiries, I never had any takers, and decided the concept was a waste of time.

To forestall further inquiries, the answer is no, I do not offer ghost tours. My initial feeling about them, and it was a good instinct, was that many of the haunted locations on Block Island are private property, and I have no wish to intrude on people's privacy or property. For that reason, I have left vague, in this collection of stories, the locations of private homes that are haunted, on the order of "somewhere on a road." That is as it should be. If ghosts need or want to materialize, they most likely will. There's no sense going hunting for them.

If someone wants to walk or bike around the Island's public byways, book in hand, and locate haunted buildings, it's good exercise. A walk around town is, too, and I've taken walks around Old Harbor with small groups of interested people and told them ghost stories. Another good exercise for people to do on their own is to go up and walk around the Island Cemetery and try to locate certain gravestones. Good luck! Whether particular stones come to light or not, there will be many other interesting ones to see, and it will be a fun walk.

I hasten to add to all of the above that I am delighted to meet people who are interested in Block Island ghosts. I've made many new friends that way.

# Acknowledgments

I AM EXTREMELY GRATEFUL TO ALL WHO HAVE HELPED, in one capacity or another, in the preparation of this book:

All of the storytellers mentioned in these pages who generously shared their ghosts and their haunts.

People at the other end of a telephone call who good-humoredly helped me with historic or current details, or who, when asked, reviewed stories prior to publication: Willis Dodge, Dub Barrows, Martha Ball, Verna Littlefield, Wendy Much Crawford, Edith Blane, Nancy Greenaway, Martha Agricola, Al Starr, Josephine Dugan, Charles Beck, Don Littlefield, Pam Littlefield Gasner, Adrian Mitchell, Maureen Quackenbush, Rita Draper, Elwin Dodge, Claire Pike, Diane Tripler, Allen Hall, Kenn Fischburg, Lew Gaffett, Vin McAloon.

People who, with unfailing good cheer and fine senses of humor, went out of their way to help me locate facts or records, or who lent props: Betty Gann, Lisa Sprague, Lisa Ommerle, Millie McGinnes, Bonny Ryan, Avery Kirby, Laurie Bertholdt Gempp, Arthur Rose.

Professionals who have lent this effort the very best of their vision, editorial input and artistic abilities: photographer Marea Mott, artist and photographer Gillian Stevens, graphic designer Susan Filippone, photographer Dave Dolan, architect and photographer Kay McManus.

Rally, for his patience.

Doglets Tia Maria and Coco Chanel, for their companionship and for getting me out of my chair and away from work when they could.

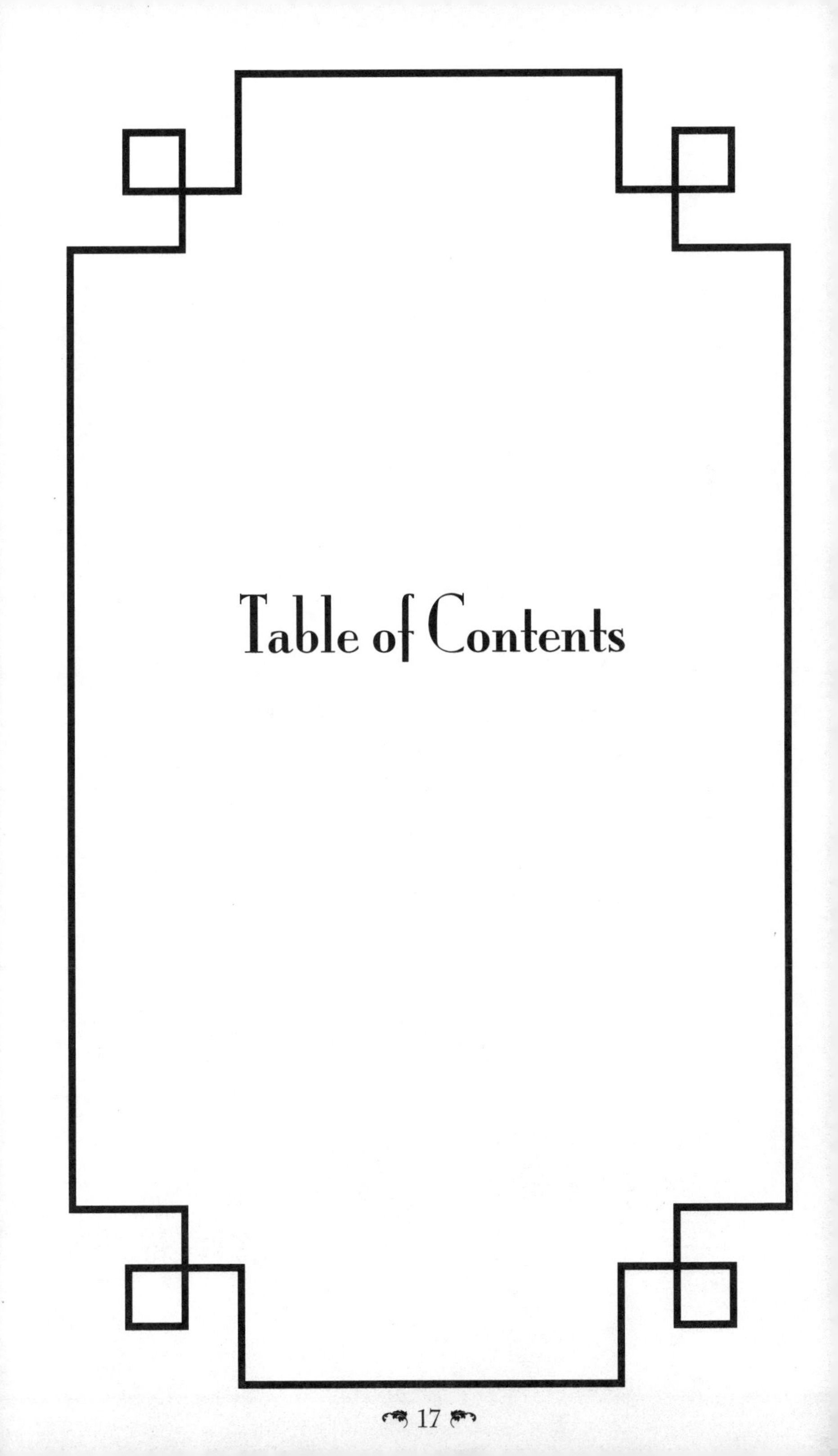

# Table of Contents

# List of Illustrations

# Ghost Rules and Ghost Etiquette

THE FOLLOWING ARE BITS OF GHOST LORE, truths perhaps, and etiquette that I have been told at various times. After reading the stories in this book, readers may decide for themselves what they think a ghost is, what a ghost can or cannot do, and how they would approach a ghost if they met one. Perhaps they will come up with their own lists of ghost rules and etiquette.

A ghost is a disembodied spirit.

A ghost cannot cross water, but can go on a boat; ships can be haunted.

A ghost cannot hurt you.

When you see a ghost, you're supposed to say, "What do you want?" (Personally, I think this challenge should be offered in only the most helpful tone of voice and with helpful intent, unless you feel threatened by a hostile-seeming ghost. A friendly ghost may take offense if challenged and just get up and leave, and then you'll never know anything.)

It is a bad idea to play with Ouija boards or hold séances in haunted houses. These activities can attract evil spirits through the portals.

It is a good idea, if inhabiting a haunted house, to bless each outside door and window with holy water to bar entry to evil spirits.

Another method is "smudging," done by burning a swatch of fragrant herbs to purify each space. This is a Native American tradition, and people who try it should educate themselves as to proper technique, or consult a qualified person

A "sensitive" is a person who can perceive ghosts with his or her senses. A "sensitive" may or may not believe in ghosts, and does not have to believe in them to experience them.

A ghost may attach itself to a person or family, and follow those people wherever they go.

Ghosts may be playful, helpful, instructive, protective, sad or happy. They may be seeking something. They may be hostile, but these are relatively rare. Again: a ghost cannot hurt you.

# The Voice in the Night, the Flames

"I HAVE A LEAD FOR YOU ON A GHOST STORY," said Arnie Flagg. I hadn't seen Arnie in years, but here he was at a little summer patio dance party at Adrian Mitchell's house in late August 2007. I'd first met Arnie in the 1980s when he had a shop at the south end of Water Street. Now he was a happily married family man, living off-Island but coming over every so often to work with builder Norris Pike.

"It happened back in the 1970s, at a house up near the airport," Arnie told me. "The person to talk to is Gillian Stevens — her parents used to own the Ragged Sailor gallery with Edie Blane's sister, Eileen. Gillian is an artist, I think she's living in Florida now."

Gillian is indeed an artist. Her meticulously crafted mixed media collages, many evoking important Block Island buildings, are sold at the Jessie Edwards Studio. Gillian lives in St. Petersburg, and readily gave me details of her ghost story when I called her at her home.

"Oh, yes, that was the house that burned down," Gillian said unhesitatingly, in a melodious voice filled with good humor. "My family thought I was crazy when I told them, that night, that there was a ghost in the house, but the local Island people weren't a bit surprised. I stood in the freezing cold that April night in 1974, shivering in my thin nightgown, while the house burned to the ground.

"The members of the Fire Department Ladies Auxiliary came to the fire with hot coffee and blankets. One of them, I remember, was Edrie Dodge. I grew up on the Island, and she served us lunch every day at the school cafeteria. She was always such fun to talk to when we visited the post office, too — a natural comedian! I loved her.

"I told members of the Ladies Auxiliary that there was a ghost in the house. Nobody looked surprised — they said it wasn't the first time that house had had a fire in it. And there was a precursor to the event."

Realizing I didn't have the whole picture, Gillian paused and backed up a bit to tell me the story of her former house, located at the end of a dead-end road, not far from the Indian Cemetery at Isaac's Corner.

"My parents were living next door to the house that burned down. My father built our house on Old Center Road, directly across the stone wall from the airport, in the 1960s. It was a Berger house, one of the first that came over on the ferryboat, and Ray Bertholdt poured the foundation. There weren't that many new houses going up on the Island back then.

"In the house just south of my parents lived an older couple named Wiggins. We called Mr. Wiggins 'Uncle Wiggily.' Apparently, the Wigginses didn't want to deal with the responsibility of an Island house any more, and in the 1970s they sold their house to my parents.

"My parents were Peter and Diana Stevens. My mother was co-owner of the Ragged Sailor gallery with Eileen Littlefield Lee, who was Edie Blane's sister. My father was a portrait painter. He spent a lot of time going back and forth to do commissioned portraits through Portraits Inc. in New York City.

"At that time, I was married to the top art director for Hallmark Cards in Kansas City, Missouri. I was back on the Island, helping my parents gut and remodel the Wiggins house for my own family. I was waiting for my husband to move here; my two stepdaughters were attending school in Missouri. I had a stepson, too, who worked on the Island during a few summers painting houses. I was twenty-six years old, and I was so excited at the prospect of having my own house on the Island.

"I could feel a presence in the house that we were gutting. My two stepdaughters, who had spent summers with me and my family for years, had always felt a presence in that house too, long before the incident I'm about to describe.

"Another person who had always felt a supernatural presence in the house was a very close friend of ours, a ballet dancer who gave ballet, yoga and jazz classes on the Island at the old Vail Hotel. Her name was Doris Driver. Judy Clark used to take her classes, I remember.

"That April afternoon in 1974, I was in Westerly with my parents, helping them buy groceries. We got back to the Island late in the day. It was my first night of moving into the Wiggins house alone, and I felt uncomfortable at the thought of sleeping upstairs in the house by myself. I told my father that I wanted to move the bedroom furnishings downstairs. So, Wayne Ritter, who was a contemporary of mine, came over and helped my father move the bedroom things downstairs. My father probably thought I was being foolish, but he moved everything, and let me tell you, it saved my life!

"When I went to bed in the house that night and got under the covers, I felt a presence in the room with me, a very definite presence. It spoke to me telepathically and said, 'Get out! I'm going to kill you! You're not wanted here!'

"There was noe one else in the house, I knew that, but the presence was unmistakable and so were the words. I lay there, having this sort of telepathic conversation with the presence, asking it why we *both* couldn't occupy the house. It was a desperate attempt on my part to mollify it, as it seemed quite hostile.

"Then I heard noises. I distinctly heard the sound of something being dropped on the porch of the south end of the house. After that, I heard crackling sounds. I got up from the bed to look out, and flames were engulfing the entire south side of the building. I went and shut off the main power switch, to avoid the spread of fire through the electrical system. Then I raced outside, ran across the wall to my parents' house. I yelled, 'The house is on fire, the house is on fire!' and I called the fire department. My dad, in the panic of getting up suddenly, ran over to the burning house in his pajamas, thinking irrationally that he had to save a cat or a dog. We didn't have any pets over there, but it just shows what a dear person my dad was, that it would be the first thing he'd think of doing.

"In those days, the calls for the fire department were received at the airport. The firemen had been fighting another fire earlier that day, and they were all downtown. By the time they could respond to the call and reach us way up at the end of Old Center Road, the flames had taken hold. It was a terrifying thing, watching them fight that fire, risking their lives to go up and chop holes on the roof. Jim Mott was the fire chief, I remember, and my brother, Brandon, and our friend, Wayne Ritter, were there helping fight the fire.

"I never mentioned the creepy feeling I had in that house to my parents until that night, and only after the house was in flames. My parents thought I'd gone 'round the bend.' They were both total skeptics, and thought I was crazy. I thought that was odd, because they were both English, and I would have expected them to have more of a feel for ghostly presences, but they didn't.

"The house couldn't be saved, in spite of the heroic efforts of the firefighters. It burned to the ground and was never rebuilt. When nothing more could be done and the fire was out, the firemen left. The chief came back later to ask questions and find out what he could about the cause. There were some interesting facts. One was that there was absolutely no electrical wiring in the end of the house where the fire had started. We'd gutted everything, and hadn't put the wiring in there yet.

"Another was that there was a professional firefighter from New Jersey who collaborated with the Block Island Fire Department to investigate the fire. The New Jersey firefighter thought the fire was caused by arson. He thought the house had been doused with gasoline or something equally flammable. The firemen thought that the noise I'd heard just before the flames, of something dropping on the porch at the south end of the house, might have been a can that had held a flammable liquid.

"After the house burned, we all went back to my parents' house, and went to bed for a few hours. We were exhausted, to say the least.

"The entity that I had encountered before the fire visited my father that very night.

"As my parents were trying to sleep, Dad felt something come into their bedroom. He said it tried to suffocate him; he felt a huge pressure weighing on his chest, and along with it he felt a sudden, unexplainable, cold clamminess in the air. Dad decided he would count to a certain number, then speak to the thing, whatever it was. So he counted, then told the presence to leave, and it did. We never felt it again after he told it to leave.

"My father told me of that frightening experience, and believed that it had been a non-human entity. My skeptical parents changed their minds pretty quickly about ghosts after that. Dad said it seemed female, and why 'she' visited him is still a mystery.

"That house, the one my parents built, is still there.

"Something else happened the day the other house burned. That afternoon, little did my parents and I know, but while we were away in Westerly, Eileen Lee drove up to our house looking for us. She told us later that she smelled a very strong odor of kerosene in the house.

"After the house burned, another friend, Geri Hutchinson, who used to have that wonderful big house right on Crescent Beach, told me she had sensed all that day that something bad would happen on the Island, she just didn't know what. Geri was very sensitive, psychic, and often had a prescience, a foreknowledge of things about to happen."

Gillian returned to something she had mentioned at the beginning of her story. "I said there was a precursor to the fire, and it was this: in my dad's house, I was lying in my bedroom and I looked up and saw a newspaper literally floating through the air above me in the room. I could see that it had bright, vivid red headlines — but I couldn't read them. I was scared, I mean who wouldn't be, seeing this red-lettered newspaper floating overhead. Several weeks later, the fire occurred in the other house.

"I think that precursor in my dad's house was a warning, and I truly think there were miracles throughout all these events. The first was that I didn't want to sleep upstairs in the gutted house the night of the fire, and that decision saved my life. The second was that the voice warned me that I could be killed; perhaps it was trying to scare me out of the house and save my life. The third was the precursor, the floating newspaper with red headlines that I think was a warning."

I had listened to Gillian's narrative over the telephone, and I felt somehow drained, just hearing the sequence of events that had threatened, yet perhaps saved, her life.

"Ghosts can't hurt you," I offered.

"But they can frighten you, and perhaps give you a warning," she replied thoughtfully, adding, "People who spend a lot of time living on Block Island, like Geri Hutchinson, seem to develop a sensitivity to ghosts. The older people on the Island always had stories of the spiritual presences that they felt or perceived. Some of the islanders knew that the Wiggins house was 'haunted,' but never said anything to my family about it as we were off-islanders."

"Ghosts can't cross water," I said, "so an island must tend to collect ghosts and keep them."

"People do say that ghosts can't cross water," Gillian replied, "but I had experiences with ghosts in New Canaan, Connecticut, too, after I left the Island, and not long after the fire. I consulted a psychic and was told there was a presence that stayed with me and haunted me. Maybe it came from Block Island. Maybe it had something to do with the house that burned. Maybe somehow it's been watching out for me.

"Some individuals attract spirits. The spirits may not actually be hostile, merely trying to gain attention for one reason or another. As I am what is referred to as a "sensitive" — I did readings for people for 10 years — it may be the reason that I've had these experiences.

"I left the Island not long after the fire, because I was so depressed. Not only did my family lose the house, but I lost all of my personal belongings, including my RISD [Rhode Island School of Design] portfolio and artwork I'd created for my stepchildren's bedrooms, which I'd lovingly fixed up for them. Artwork I'd bought from other Island artists at the Ragged Sailor, like Sandra Swan's and Eileen and John Lee's, also burned.

"As I said, I was so excited about having my own Island home. It was too much to bear when my dream died. The only good that came out of it all was the spiritual lesson I learned, which was not to be attached to material things. A difficult lesson, but an invaluable one."

# The Spirit at the Fork in the Road

PEOPLE SOMETIMES WONDER IF ANIMALS GO TO "HEAVEN," or if animals have souls. I often wonder why people wonder these things. I believe that animals are not only loving, but telepathic, even mystical. Their senses are heightened far beyond the abilities of our own, and perhaps this sensitivity extends to their perceptions of the supernatural as well. Perhaps, as suggested by the teller of the following story, human spirits can take animal form.

Hope Day Pilkington, who lives in Edgewood, Rhode Island, wrote to me in 2006 with an account of two "odd experiences" she had while visiting a certain spot on Block Island. Mrs. Pilkington, now 70, vacationed here as a child with her family in the 1940s.

Her father, Harrison J. Day, born in Providence on August 1, 1903, was brought to the Island by his parents each summer for weeks at a time during his childhood, along with his sister, Hope Day McDonald. As Hope Day Pilkington writes, "They were such regular visitors that lifelong friendships were established with Island residents."

One of Mrs. Pilkington's own most memorable vacations to the Island with her parents occurred in 1949:

"In 1949 we rented a little house down the street from Tom, Esther and Murtis Littlefield for a three-week vacation, August 14 to Labor Day," she wrote. "Tom Littlefield was my father's dear childhood friend.

"The house stood on the fork of the road between Connecticut Avenue and Old Town Road. It was owned by Amy MacDonald, the smallest, most wrinkled witch-like person I had ever seen — and lovely to sit and talk with. She sat with us talking brilliantly. I remembered her telling us that she had to swim at night because the children made fun of her. How sad! She lived upstairs with another tenant — Mrs. Brown, "Brownie," from New York.

"We had an idyllic week. My father had returned to Providence; he was an executive with Narragansett Electric. We four Day kids — Barbara, 15; me, 11; Eleanor, 8; and Harrison Day Jr., 2 — together with our cousin Diane and our mother, spent lovely days at the beach, went to the movies at night, and took scary streetlight-less walks home afterward.

"We picked blackberries near the High View, and three of us — Eleanor, Diane and I — sat on the hedge across the street each time we walked by it. It survived us!

"On Friday evening, my father came back to the Island. The next day, my Aunt Hope came to collect Diane. We all went down to Old Harbor to greet her. Aunt Hope was part of the crowd leaving the boat, when my father chimed in with the hotel drivers who called out the names of their hotels. He shouted "SURF!" in his booming voice. We couldn't yet see Aunt Hope, but over the crowd came her burst of laughter. It was their private joke — the Surf Hotel, in 1949, had been closed for years.

"We had a beautiful day. My father drove us all around his beloved Island, giving us a wonderful tour. After Aunt Hope and Diane returned to the mainland we had supper, a traditional New England franks and beans. During dinner my father announced that he wanted to retire to Block Island. My mother laughed and said, "You'll do it alone!"

"That night, August 20, 1949, my father suffered a fatal heart attack. He was 46.

"The next day was a blur: Tom and Esther Littlefield packing our things — a tearful Sunday Mass — Murtis Littlefield trying to tempt us to eat breakfast at their house — they had blackberries and I could not eat them, because at 11 years of age, I thought my father had died of blackberry poisoning from eating the berries we had picked. Amy MacDonald refusing to take any rent money — the private room on the boat — the silent crowd on the dock as we followed the casket off the boat: there was total silence as our young, bereaved family walked off the boat with the casket. My mother, the young widow, was only 42 years old. And the ride to Providence in "one of *those* cars." Tom Littlefield later served as a pallbearer at my father's funeral.

"Life had changed forever.

"We grew up. We survived.

"Barbara and Ellie became RNs, Harry is in the jewelry business, Diane and I are both retired elementary school teachers. We all have families, lovely homes, college degrees. Aunt Hope passed away at 80 with her coat on and car keys in her hand. Always on the go! Our mother — strong, bright, and elegant, died in her sleep. She lived a healthy life, outliving our father by 49 years!

"The little house with the red peeling paint is no longer there. Just the stairs and foundation remain…and a bench.

"Twice I have had very odd experiences there.

"Four years ago on a day trip, in 2002, I decided to walk up the hill to the site. I sat on the bench, I said a little prayer and then it started to rain. It wasn't pouring, but the little sprinkle that gently kisses your cheek announcing what's coming. Great — I had no umbrella or transportation, just visions of a soaked tourist taking the early boat. Wanting to beat the rain to town, I crossed the road.

"There *was* no rain, then or for the rest of the day.

"Just the memory of my kissed cheek.

"The next year I repeated my trip. No clouds this time. That same huge hedge that we used to sit on as children was still in the same place, and flourishing. It certainly did survive.

"I walked up to the bench and as I sat down I noticed two cats sitting upright in the driveway across Connecticut Avenue, watching me. Suddenly, one of them — a straggling yellow Tom — dashed into the street just as two cars passed each other. The road is narrow, and the running cat crossed the street escaping all eight tires.

"He hopped up on the embankment, up on the bench, and into my lap.

"Visions of deer ticks, fleas, rabies and dealing with an unruly feral cat who was sitting in my lap curled up and acting as though he was mine, rather startled me. Cats, even ones who know you, don't do this. He did, and he stayed. People walked by. He stayed. Afraid to offend my visitor, I sat. He stayed. A woman walked by. I told her that he jumped into my lap.

"Well, enjoy it," she said.

"You have no idea, I thought.

"I talked to my visitor in my "nice kitty" voice, all the while wondering if cats have spirit friends, or do spirits take cat forms? After awhile, common sense and the uncomfortable feeling that this was somewhat supernatural made me decide I'd had enough. I told the cat that I was sorry I had to leave, but I'd be back.

"And he got down. He watched me with the saddest eyes as I walked away. I can't explain it and really don't want to. It was quite lovely and I felt blessed.

"After I read your book I began to wonder. Perhaps the Days do inhabit the High View and they have a tenant — my father."

The first owner of the High View, as mentioned in *Ghosts of Block Island*, was M.M. Day. The High View, then called the Connecticut House, was built in 1878, and M.M. Day died a few years later. The property passed to his widow, Joannah, and his son.

Jennie Day is mentioned, in Fred Benson's 1977 book, *Research, Reflection and Recollections of Block Island*, as an early owner of the Connecticut House, now known as the High View.

Hope Day Pilkington wrote, "Jennie Day often called my father.

They were not relatives, but were good friends from my father's childhood of Island visits." She also said that as far as she knew, her father was unrelated to M.M. Day.

The tiny lot where the bench now stands is co-owned by abutting neighbor Cliff McGinnes and an owner on the mainland. The little house with peeling red paint that once stood there, in which Hope Day Pilkington's father died that night in 1949, burned down. Old Town Road neighbor Verna Littlefield places the fire in the 1970s.

"It burned on Thanksgiving Day," Verna said decisively. "Dr. Much was here with his family, having dinner with us, and he looked out the window and said, 'You didn't have to provide entertainment, too!' He was our Island school superintendent then."

Wendy Much Crawford, Dr. Much's daughter, was at that Thanksgiving dinner and was a young teenager. She places the year at 1981, because she was in eighth grade at the time. Wendy added, "There were actually two fires in that house: one in the 1970s, and the later one in 1981 that burned the rest of the house down."

So, Verna and Wendy are both right.

The driveway across Connecticut Avenue from the bench where Hope Day Pilkington sat with the mysterious yellow cat on her lap belongs to Lonni Todd, founder of the Block Island Volunteers for Animals. The organization sponsors a spaying, neutering and adoption program for the Island's burgeoning feral cat population. It is no surprise that there are cats at Lonni's house, but they are generally confined to a fenced-in back yard. It is unusual for them to be outside the gate, though there are one or two who have the strength, agility and determination to leap and scale the tall fence.

Perhaps that particular yellow Tom was waiting there, that day, for a very special visitor to arrive at the bench, someone he was expecting. And maybe he brought a long-time neighborhood friend with him, to help him keep watch and pass the time of day.

SURF HOTEL

# Spirits Away at the Surf, and Bedtime at Lorraine's

THE DIMINUTIVE, ENERGETIC LADY of 70-something stood purposefully at my book-selling table at the Block Island Arts and Crafts Guild Fair, the Saturday of Columbus Day weekend, 2008.

"I have a ghost story," she said. She looked me in the eye: her gaze direct, her smile intent. She nodded her head vigorously. She wore a stylishly autumnal knit jacket of purplish tweed, and her gray hair danced with the motion of her head.

Her name, she told me, was Gladys Kruchok. She had been a regular guest at the Surf Hotel for many summers and, like so many of the Surf regulars, had formed a strong friendship with owners Ulric and Beatrice Cyr and their daughter, Lorraine.

Gladys was on the Island that summer weekend to visit with the Cyrs. It was the first summer season after Bea and Ulric had closed the doors of their beloved Surf Hotel, and put it on the market. With the grand, quirky old building standing empty, a "For Sale" sign nailed to its front, Gladys was one of many former Surf guests who felt disoriented, longing for the hospitality and welcoming cheer that the Cyrs had extended to guests and friends since they opened their hotel on July 4, 1956.

"I used to have Room 37," Gladys told me. "Before I took it over, the Lambs always had that room." She was referring to Diane and David Lamb, the owners of Lamb's Package Service, who had stayed at the Surf for years before they decided to buy a house on Block Island and start their business here.

"This was years ago," Gladys said. "I used to do arts and crafts with a friend of mine, and one day we were downstairs at the Surf, making our lavalieres. One of us needed a particular kind of cord, so I went back up to Room 37 to get it.

"When I'd left the room that morning, I'd left our supply of that particular cord on top of a bag, on the bed. But when I went up to look for it, only the bag was there. It was where I'd left it, but the supply of cord was gone.

"We turned the hotel upside down! We knew the cord had to be somewhere, and we looked every place we could think of but didn't find it.

"Three hours later, my friend and I went back into Room 37. Our supply of cord was back on top of the bag, right where I'd left it, as if it had been untouched. It hadn't been there before, and nobody else had gone in or out of the room between then and the time we found it there.

"My friend would never go in Room 37 again," Gladys concluded.

I saw Diane and David Lamb about a month later at the 89th birthday party of Ulric Cyr, the owner of the Surf Hotel. They remembered Room 37 very well, though they had never had ghosts there, they told me.

"We had Room 37 for five years at the Surf before we decided to move to the Island," Diane told me. "We stayed there by chance one summer after the previous person had died. Before that, we'd always had another room. When Room 37 became available, before the start of the season, Lorraine moved our reservation there.

"It's the best room in the house! It's on the third floor, a corner room overlooking the water, with a living room and its own bathroom. We couldn't believe our good luck, and asked Lorraine about moving our reservation. She told us we could have been trading up all those years! So, we stayed in Room 37 for the next five years. We used the living room as our hospitality suite — everyone had little parties going on in their rooms, and we all knew each other — it was like a big family!"

After describing her experience with Room 37 at the Surf, Gladys Kruchok also told me that she'd had an odd experience in Lorraine Cyr's house. This didn't surprise me; Lorraine herself had told me of eerie occurrences, as detailed in *Ghosts of Block Island*, experienced by herself and others in her relatively new house on Ocean Avenue,.

Said Gladys, "I was staying at Lorraine's house, on the second floor. In those days I had long hair, and I used very large bobby pins to hold it in place. When I went to bed, I would leave the bobby pins and an elastic on the dresser next to the bed.

"The night I was there, I got up in the middle of the night to use the bathroom. I got back into bed, and as I was lying there, trying to get back to sleep, I felt the edge of the bed go down. There was a lot of weight on it, and it was definitely the feel of someone else getting into the bed.

"I was scared — too scared to say anything, too scared to look! I should have screamed, or said something, but I just couldn't.

"But nothing happened, and I went back to sleep.

"The next morning, when I got ready to do up my hair for the day, I went to the dresser where I'd left my bobby pins and the elastic. The elastic was there, in the middle of the dresser, and the bobby pins were arranged around it like a sunburst! I certainly hadn't left them that way the night before — but something, or someone else, had!"

As mentioned in the chapter on Lorraine's house in *Ghosts of Block Island,* Lorraine had told me that "her friend Gladys," who stayed in the house for a week one February, heard something tapping on the wall, two nights in a row during her stay. Gladys had said it sounded like Morse code, and wished she had a code book to decipher it.

Another person who felt someone get into her bed in the middle of the night at Lorraine's house was Lorraine's cousin, Beatrice, a chambermaid at the Surf Hotel. While waiting for her husband, the hotel night watchman, to return home after his shift, she heard someone come into the room. Assuming it was her husband, she complained to him about the noisy flapping of the window shades when he entered the room. He said nothing, and she felt him get into bed.

Awhile later, Beatrice got up to use the bathroom. When she returned to bed, no one was there, nor was there any sign that anyone had been there. It was only 2:00 a.m., too early for her husband to be off his watch — yet she knew someone had come into the room and gotten into bed.

As for the sunburst of bobby pins, maybe they were arranged by the same admiring entity that left a silver bracelet on a dresser in the room of Karen Nyzio, Lorraine's niece, one winter when Lorraine and Karen were the only two people in the house. Neither of them had ever seen the bracelet before, neither knew where it had come from — but there it was, where it had not been before.

# Those Reappearing Shells in the Surf

PEG O'LOUGHLIN CALLED ME ON THE PHONE one afternoon in 2005, after the publication of *Ghosts of Block Island.* "Once when I was a little girl, I was marching in a parade with my sister in Stonington, Connecticut," she began. "It was a VJ Day parade."

VJ Day, or Victory over Japan Day, once celebrated as a holiday all over the country and in other WWII allied countries, is now celebrated in this country only by Rhode Island. The name of the holiday, now the Monday of a three-day weekend, has been altered to Victory Day. The actual date of VJ Day is August 14, 1945, and the holiday falls on either the second or third weekend of August.

Peg continued, "As my sister and I were marching in the parade, we both saw my grandmother waving to us. I noticed that she was wearing a pretty pink dress, with blue satin trim.

"Later that day, I told my mother about it. She said, 'Oh, you couldn't have seen her. She died, honey — don't you remember?'

"Yes, I did remember: my grandmother had just died. But I'd seen her, I knew I had, and I described to my mother the dress she'd been wearing.

"My mother listened, and then told me: just that morning, she had picked out that very same dress for my grandmother to be buried in.

"My sister and I both saw our grandmother, and we both saw her in the pink dress.

"My mother said to us, 'Don't tell anyone you saw your grandmother — they'll think you have the evil eye!' She said it in Portuguese, 'Mau olhado.'

"But that's not why I'm calling you," Peg said, having commanded my full interest and attention. She continued:

"One day, years ago when we first moved here, I was helping Lillian get the Surf open." Peg was referring to Lillian Martin, the vivacious sister of Surf Hotel owner Beatrice Cyr. Lillian helped her sister and brother-in-law, Ulric Cyr, run the Surf during their 51 years in business.

"I ended up working at the Surf that summer, too," Peg said. "That was in 1992 or '93 — we moved to the Island in 1992.

"Anyway, one day before the season started, while I was helping Lillian open up, I was vacuuming the second floor hallway. I was up there all by myself.

"I noticed a line of little pebbly-like shells on the floor, and I vacuumed them up. I moved on, and I looked back where I'd vacuumed. The shells had reappeared!

"So, I vacuumed them up again.

"And they reappeared again — in front of me!

"Well, I was getting a little tired of that game, so I just said, 'Hey — I'm cleaning your hotel! Cut out the comedy!'

"And it stopped. I vacuumed the shells for a third time, and after that, they didn't come back.

"Another time at the Surf, I was looking down the stairs from the second floor, all the way to the bottom, past the front desk, to the door on the right that goes into the dining room. I saw a lady in a costume — it looked Victorian to me — sitting in a rocking chair in front of that door. And I said to myself, 'Oh there's a lady in a costume down there, that's odd.' Later, I mentioned it to Lorraine."

Lorraine Cyr, one of Bea and Ulric Cyr's two daughters, always worked at the hotel for her parents. From the time I first came to the Island, in 1986, she took room reservations for the hotel all winter, presided at the front desk and managed the hotel all summer. Until, that is, the Cyrs retired and closed the doors of their beloved hotel, after the 2007 summer season.

Peg continued her story: "I told Lorraine, 'There's somebody down there in a costume — what's going on?'

"'There is?' Lorraine asked. 'Where do you see this?'

"So I told her that this lady in a Victorian costume was sitting in the rocking chair in front of the door to the dining room in the downstairs hall.

"'There's no rocking chair in that hall!' Lorraine said.

"I insisted, 'But I saw this lady in a rocking chair down there, in that spot.'

"Finally, she said, 'Oh, you probably saw Aunt Jennie!'"

I've known Peg and Jim O'Loughlin since the late 1980s, shortly after I moved to the Island. Rally and I met them at the summer socials once held at St. Andrew parish center by members of the parish. The socials were potluck hors d'oeuvres get-togethers, with soft drinks and a small bar set up on the deck overlooking the ocean. Anyone who wanted to go was welcome; we always saw plenty of people we knew, and met plenty of interesting new people and visitors to the Island as well.

The O'Loughlins were still living in Westford, Massachusetts in those days and spending weekends at their home on the Island's west side. Jim, an engineer by profession, had a boat. Like most engineers, he delighted in having projects to putter with, and the boat was one of them. Peg's background was in nursing. When Jim retired from his engineering job, the O'Loughlins moved to the Island full time. Peg joined the Ecumenical Choir, and another of Jim's projects became overseeing the sound systems used for music at St. Andrew Church on Chapel Street in the summer and at the Parish Center on Spring Street in the winter. Eventually, Jim inherited from someone else the job of coordinating the mikes and speakers used in the variety shows, known as the Summer Extravaganzas, that the Ecumenical Choir produced for years.

Peg and Jim raised three children, and are staunch churchgoers and professional people of the pragmatic "real world." Yet, as Peg let me know with her opening story, she has always been sensitive to supernatural presences.

As for the Aunt Jennie in the rocking chair, she is Jennie Day, the aunt of Almeida Day Littlefield Rose. Almeida died when Lorraine Cyr was 22, in 1968; the Cyr family, Lorraine told me, was very close to Almeida. One of Almeida's grandmothers owned the Ocean View, and the other owned the Surf.

The Cyrs didn't know much about Aunt Jennie, though Beatrice Cyr described her to me as, "Very stern, very mannish, and never married."

A further, brief notation on Jennie Day, establishing her connection with the Surf Hotel, was sent to me in 2006 by Hope Day Pilkington, who lives in Edgewood, Rhode Island, and has wonderfully vivid memories of vacationing on the Island as a child with her parents during the 1940s. She wrote:

"My father, Harrison J. Day, was born in Providence on August 1, 1903. Each summer during his childhood, his parents, his sister Hope, and he, vacationed for weeks at a time on Block Island.

"They were such regular visitors that lifelong relationships were established with Island residents.

"As a child I can recall many phone calls from the Island. My father's dear childhood friend, Tom Littlefield, and an older woman would frequently call. Her name was Jennie Day. She had something to do with a hotel — owned the Surf, I think."

"I remember Aunt Jennie Day!" Claire Slate Pike told me one evening in late November 2008, when I was visiting her about another ghost. Claire is a Dodge on her mother's side, and has an encyclopedic memory of the Island as it was when she grew up here. She told me, "Aunt Jennie wore big earrings that sat on her shoulders. She had the Surf, back in the days when we young girls used to go out dancing on summer evenings. I used to go out with two or three friends, and we were always welcome at the hotel dances. We'd go to the National, and after it closed at 10:00 we'd go over to the Surf.

"Aunt Jennie was always there, and she called it 'her' dance hall. Sometimes she seemed glad to see us, sometimes not. She'd always say, 'Now you girls behave yourselves in my dance hall! No one goes out on the porch, do you understand?!' She was very stern!"

An owner as vigilant as Aunt Jennie would of course post herself, even in her afterlife, in a chair at a doorway at her hotel — near the front door, of course, so she could watch all comings and goings. She might also keep track of the housekeeping, making sure that everything was cleaned just so, perhaps testing the help by leaving something on the floor to see if it would be vacuumed as it should be.

# Lorraine's Levitating Spaniels

"I HAVE ANOTHER STORY ABOUT MY HOUSE that I never told you," said Lorraine Cyr to me one evening in her kitchen. It was November 8, 2008, the 89th birthday of Lorraine's father, Ulric Cyr. Lorraine, her mother Beatrice, and her aunt Lillian Martin, had all put on a surprise birthday party for Ulric at Lorraine's house, with family and close friends to help celebrate. Lorraine had made lots of pizzas, designed to satisfy every conceivable taste in toppings, and there was a decorated birthday cake with candles (but not 89) for dessert.

Lorraine is a breeder of Cavalier King Charles spaniels, and four adult dogs joined the festivities and kept an eye on the floor-cleaning detail. Two six-week-old puppies, Honeysuckle and Rosa Rugosa, slept in the next room, with occasional toddling, sleepy forays out of bed. Guests took turns holding the plump, soft little bundles.

Ulric, who had had his share of health issues that year, was looking robust and happy. He was looking forward to a trip with Bea to Florida, leaving in January to spend the rest of the winter in sunny St. Petersburg.

"This happened sometime in the mid-1990s," Lorraine prefaced her story. "You had already written that other story about the ghosts in this house and put it in *The Block Island Times*, so I didn't bother to mention it to you."

She continued, "I had one particular dog at that time, a male black-and-tan King Charles. I don't remember his name, but I remember his barking! He had a barking habit, and he often barked while we were in the house, when there seemed to be nothing there. Sometimes he'd bark at night, and that was annoying.

"One night he was sleeping in my room with me and he started barking in the middle of the night and then left the bed. I don't know when, exactly, all I know is that I got up to use the bathroom and found the dog on top of the bathroom vanity, next to the sink! He was very frightened, and shivering, and he whimpered at me when I came into the room.

"I took him down from the sink, because he couldn't get down by himself.

"He couldn't have gotten up there by himself, either! Dogs, especially ones as small as a Cavalier King Charles, can't jump that high, and there was nothing for him to jump on top of that would get him up to that sink! There was no logical way for him to be there — but he was there, and he was horribly frightened of something!

"I think he was barking at the ghost in the house, and the ghost got annoyed," Lorraine concluded matter-of-factly. She continued:

"A few years later, the exact same thing happened with another dog. She was that dog's granddaughter. She had a barking habit, too, and one night I found her up on that same sink, as frightened as she could be!

"Neither of those dogs ever barked at night again, after they found themselves on top of my bathroom sink in the middle of the night — something really gave them a good scare!"

When Lorraine has guests at her house, she tells them to put their coats in her bedroom, on the bed. Rally had a fleece jacket, the evening of Ulric's birthday party, and Lillian Martin had put it in there when we arrived. When we were ready to leave, we went in the bedroom to retrieve the jacket.

"I want to look in the bathroom," I told him, opening the door of the bathroom that adjoins Lorraine's bedroom.

I looked to the right, at the sink and vanity. The bathtub was directly across from the vanity, on the other side of the room. The toilet was beyond the tub, in the corner. There was nothing near the vanity or sink — no stool, no other bathroom appliance — that would enable a small, low-built dog to ascend to the height of the vanity top all by itself. Nothing whatsoever.

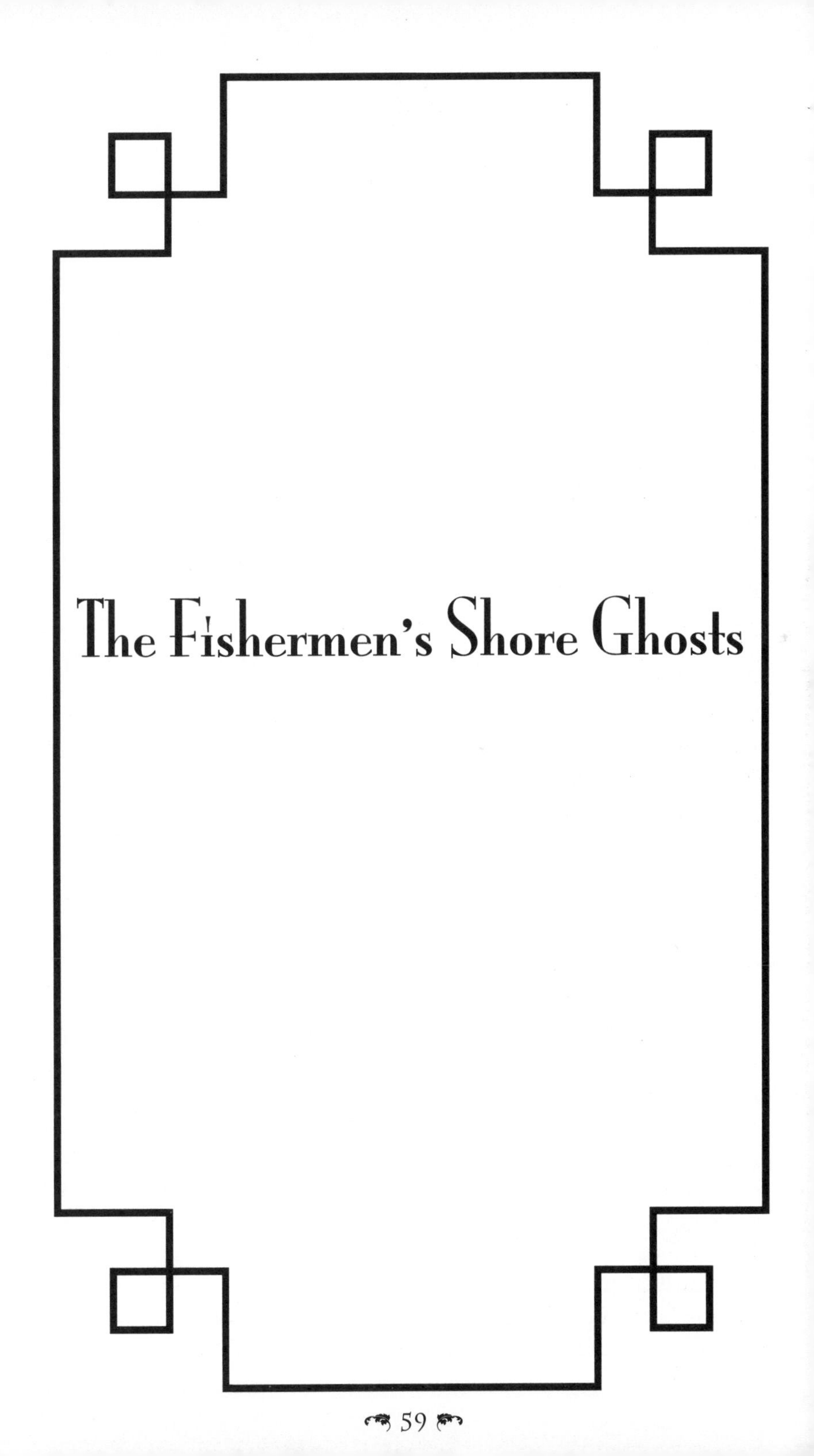

# The Fishermen's Shore Ghosts

AN E-MAIL CORRESPONDENT whom I knew only as Shawn for two years contacted me in January 2007 to pose a question: "I stayed in a house on Block Island several years ago. It was located on a hill overlooking the harbor. We heard strange noises all night and later were told that the home was haunted. Since then, a friend told me the home was on the cover of a book. Does this sound like your book?" — It was signed, "Shawn."

Well, not exactly. My book certainly did have a haunted house on the cover, and it is on relatively high ground, but any harbor — in that case, New Harbor — can be viewed only at a distance, from a second or third story window.

I wrote as much to Shawn. He persisted in trying to locate his haunted house on a hill overlooking the harbor where his friend's boat was berthed. He unearthed a picture and attached it to an e-mail — Eureka! — no, actually, not the old Eureka Hotel at all, but the MacGregor house, beautifully situated between Town Beach and the Great Salt Pond, high on a hill. After I'd identified the house for Shawn, he told me his story:

"I visited Block Island in 1995 to go fishing. A friend had his boat there for a week or so. I live in Maryland so another friend and myself flew up and landed on the grass runway on the Island.

"Our cab driver drove an old Chevy station wagon and loaded up our bags. As soon as we gave him the address where we were staying, he commented, "That is the haunted house." We laughed it off.

"That evening we went to dinner at a nice restaurant on the harbor and you could see the home from our table. We told our friends the story at dinner and one of them asked the waitress if she knew anything about the house on the hill. She replied it was haunted. We laughed again.

"That evening, we went back to the house. It had two bedrooms at the top of the stairs. My friend Gary stayed in one, I stayed in the other. We had gone to bed around 10:00 or 11:00 p.m.

"Shortly after, I heard voices and noises downstairs. It sounded like doors opening and closing. I got up and went downstairs — I thought Gary was downstairs. But when I went down, there was nothing. Nobody there.

"Gary heard the same noises. He got up and thought it was me downstairs. It was kind of an uneasy feeling, but we smiled and went back to bed.

"Later that night, around 2:00 or 3:00 a.m., noises woke me up. It sounded like a party going on downstairs. I stayed in bed and just listened, but I didn't get up again. It was a long night!

"The next morning we discussed it. He had heard the noises too. We agreed the house was creepy. The wind had kicked up and the seas were too rough to fish. We left and I have not been back since then."

In a later message, Shawn wrote, "I told my friend that I made contact with you. He looked at me and said he will never ever forget that night we stayed in the MacGregor House. That was one heck of a weird night we stayed there."

I drafted Shawn's account into a story and e-mailed it to him, almost two years after I'd received it. He replied:

"The night on Block Island recently came up in discussion at a football party. My friend Gary and I tell the story and people tend to look at us kind of odd. I find many people just smile and laugh about ghosts. They are the people who've never had an experience with any ghosts. The evening I spent on Block Island was no laughing matter. You wouldn't smile and laugh if a burglar was in your house.

"The difference was that I was not in my own home, and had no shotgun to confront the intruder or burglar in the middle of the night. Looking back, it wouldn't have mattered, shotgun or not — when I walked downstairs there was nobody to confront! Strange, but that is the only way I can explain the feeling as I lay in bed and listened to them on the first floor below me. A scary, uneasy feeling in the middle of the night, and no way to defend myself from the invisible intruder.

"The ghosts never came upstairs — as far as I know — just made themselves at home, walking and talking around the first floor of the house.

"Maybe we were the intruders — not them?"

He concluded, "Take care."

This time, the mysterious Shawn signed his full name, "Capt. Shawn R. Bennett."

The MacGregor House was built as the George W. Willis House in about 1887. It is described, in the book *Historic and Architectural Resources of Block Island, Rhode Island*, as "A bell-cast-mansard cottage with a circumferential porch, probably a later addition. Its form is interesting in counterpoint to the adjacent 'Ninicroft Lodge.'"

Ninicroft Lodge was the original name of the current Sullivan House B&B.

The George W. Willis house, now known as the MacGregor house, stands to the south of the Sullivan House and has, since 1992, been owned by the O'Brien family. The O'Briens have always referred to it as "Grandma MacGregor's."

The O'Briens are also the owners of the nearby Sullivan House.

The MacGregor house was at one time owned by Mary M. Boles. In 1927, it was conveyed to Helen M. Sullivan, and she transferred it to Mary MacGregor, of Pittsfield, Massachusetts, in 1932. The property was eventually inherited from the MacGregor estate by Mary MacGregor's descendants, Thomas, Philip and Rosalie O'Brien.

The O'Briens of Pittsfield — the parents of Thomas, Philip and Rosalie — were summer residents of Indian Neck. They were related not only to Mary MacGregor, but also to the Sullivan family, for whom the adjacent Sullivan House is currently named.

The young Thomas D. O'Brien and a much-younger neighbor child on Block Island, Ellen Ball, knew each other as youngsters. Ellen Ball was the daughter of E. Searles Ball, a Block Island plumber and fisherman, and Gertrude Ball, a primary school and music teacher at Block Island School for many years. Ellen grew up on the hill of Indian Neck in the house to the north of the Sullivan House. In 1966, she married Tom O'Brien, "the boy next door." He became an attorney in Boston. The couple had three children during their 23 years of marriage.

Ellen Ball O'Brien died in 2008 at the age of 67. She had a distinguished career as a teacher in Boston, and was a leading philanthropist and business owner on Block Island. Her husband, Tom, at the height of a successful law career in Boston, predeceased her in 1989.

In 1992, the MacGregor house became the property of Ellen Ball O'Brien, and it is now owned by Ellen and Tom's three children: Philip Ball O'Brien; Michael MacGregor O'Brien; and Rosalie O'Brien Kivlehan, who with her husband, Sean Kivlehan, is proprietor of the O'Brien family's Sullivan House on Indian Neck.

The marriage of Ellen Ball to Thomas D. O'Brien united two prominent families on Indian Neck. It is interesting to note that the Sullivan House, named for the Sulllivan relatives of Thomas O'Brien's family, was built in 1904 by Simon R. Ball, a forebear of Ellen Ball O'Brien.

I had heard no stories in my years here from Ellen, Tom, or any of their three children, that might explain the presence of ghosts in Grandma MacGregor's house. At the same time, I had no doubt as to the veracity of Shawn and Gary's story.

I was reckoning without my husband, Rally. When I happened to mention the MacGregor house to him, he said enthusiastically, "Oh, we used to go to the MacGregor house a lot in the 60s and 70s! Every year, the O'Briens and Grandma MacGregor had a big party up at that house. Phil, Tom, Rosalie and Rolt Smith, their daughter Emily, their son Rolt Jr., they were all there! Grandma MacGregor was a little tiny gray-haired woman, very charming!

"It was the party of the year, and very few people outside the family were invited."

I recalled the words of Rolt Smith Jr.'s e-mail to me in August 2008, telling us that his uncle, Phil O'Brien, had died. Rolt had written, "Your husband Rally is an old friend of my family's. I have very fond memories of Rally and my uncle and my parents at many social gatherings on the Island during my childhood."

It is wonderful to think that those great get-togethers of the 1960s and 70s are still going on up in the MacGregor house, with at least some of the same participants, and maybe previous generations of others. The members of that family would be the nicest spirits imaginable — and it's a great spot for a party.

# Visitations from Smoky Shroud and Hobnails

"THERE'S GEORGE CLARKE AT THE BAR," Rally told me, giving me a characteristic nudge on the arm. It was the end of summer, 2007, and we were sitting at our corner high-top table at The Oar, ordering lunch. We're lucky: our summer career at the Block Island Boat Basin means that we eat lunch at The Oar just about every day. We sit at our usual table inside the bar, grab a salad or sandwich, watch boaters at the dock just miss our pilings (or not miss them, as the case may be), and observe summer vacationers and cottagers lining up for tables on the deck. More often than not, a cluster of other working Island friends show up at our table for some informational exchange about everything, or nothing much, depending. Then it's back to work at our office next door, above the marina store. That's our working lunch, and everyone should be so lucky.

Rally nudged my arm again. Yes, it was George Clarke, tall and big and tanned, sitting at the bar with his wife, Anni, drinking a Barbados rum and Coke and ordering a lobster roll. He looked around.

"Rally! Fran! How are you?" he roared with a huge smile, and hurried over. I hadn't seen George in about 14 years; when I moved to Block Island in 1987, he owned a picturesque old farmhouse on Corn Neck Road with a handful of outbuildings including the old privy, and a great view of the Great Salt Pond. A cottage had been added to the property in 1960. George had bought his house in 1983. He lived on the mainland but spent R&R time on Block Island at all seasons of the year, mostly on weekends.

George sold his Block Island property in 1995 and relocated to Florida, then moved with Anni to Barbados, where he had grown up. The two have been there ever since, and now own a 100-year-old plantation house that they run as a B&B. Known as Sweetfield Manor, it is located in St. Michael.

"I have a story for you!" George said, as he arrived at our lunch table at The Oar. He and Anni were on Block Island for the Spring House wedding of John and Barbara Hirsch's daughter, and they were renting a bungalow from Ellen Ball O'Brien on Indian Neck, down Corn Neck Road a good way south from George's old house. George hadn't changed a bit in the years since I'd seen him.

"When I bought my house on the Neck from Dr. Dubois, there were rumors of ghosts," George began. "They were supposedly ghosts of the Rose family, I'm not sure why.

"One night in the dead of winter, I was alone in the house. I slept in the bedroom upstairs, and I woke up at 2:00 a.m. I felt a presence, and I thought there was something or someone in the bathroom downstairs.

"I looked through the door of the bedroom, and in the hallway was a white, misty figure. It was definitely a man, and he definitely had a beard. From the waist down, he had the appearance of a smoky shroud — I don't know how else to describe it, except that he had no legs, it was more like an indistinct form, with some swirling movement.

"I talked to myself: 'George. You haven't been drinking. Is this a dream?' I pinched myself to find out. It hurt. I looked again, and the man with the beard and the shroud was still there.

"I didn't want to go downstairs to find out if there was really something or someone in the bathroom. There was enough for me, right there in the hallway upstairs. I pulled the covers over my head and went back to sleep.

"Before that incident, there was another odd thing that happened to me in that house:

"It was in February, and there had been a huge snowstorm. Corn Neck Road was closed as far as Corn Neck Farm, and there were six-foot snowdrifts at my house.

"Nobody was around. A renter named Guy Pila had been living in the cottage at my place, but he'd left that day for the mainland. He had an old blue pickup truck. There wasn't much to do, I couldn't go anyplace, so I decided to clean the basement of the main house.

"I was down in the cellar, working, and I heard boots above me in the kitchen. Somebody was clomping around up there, and it sounded like hobnail boots. They were walking right over my head.

"I shouted, 'Guy!' thinking that Guy Pila must have come back home, maybe decided not to go to the mainland after all. There was no answer.

"I went upstairs. There was no one in the kitchen. I looked out each door of the house: the back, the front, the side. You know what my house was like, a traditional farmhouse layout.

"As I said, there were snowdrifts all around my house. I looked out every side, every door — and there were no footsteps visible, anywhere. No sign of any boot tracks. No sign of any living thing, human or animal, having entered the property: just untouched, drifted snow, all over the yard, right up to the doors."

Intrigued by George's reference to Rose family ghosts, I checked out the house's history. I called my friend Arthur Rose, 87 years old in 2008.

"It's an old house," Arthur allowed. "Been there as long as I can remember. It used to belong to Gene Rose."

The house, built in 1911, was first owned by Samuel Martin Rose and Ella G. Rose, who deeded it to Eugene L. Rose and Lenia L. Rose in 1917.

Arthur continued, "Bob Eldridge used to take care of Gene Rose before he died, and Gene left the house to him.

"I used to work for Bob Eldridge," added Arthur. "He was an electrician, and I did electrical work for him." For most of the years I have known Arthur, he served as the town's electrical inspector.

Robert Eldridge and his wife, Eva Lillian, assumed ownership of the Corn Neck Road farmhouse in 1970, and in 1981 it was sold to Dr. John J. and Adrienne DuBois, from whom George Clarke bought it in 1983.

I asked Arthur one more question. "George Clarke said there were rumors of Rose family ghosts in that house. Have you ever heard of any?"

Arthur replied with a decided, "No — none that I know of!"

So, the ghosts in the Corn Neck farmhouse may not be Roses — but, according to George Clarke, they were there — and perhaps still are — as certainly as the tracks of snow on that February day were *not* there.

# Holly and Dave and the Beach Ghost

I MET THE YOUNG COUPLE at an Arts and Crafts Guild Fair on Block Island in August 2008. Their names are Holly and Dave, and they were pushing their bikes through the arts and crafts booths on the lawn of the Block Island Historical Society. They wore light backpacks, and Velcro-fastened slings that held Nalgene water bottles. They stopped in front of my table.

"Do you know anything about ghosts on the beach?" Holly asked me, smoothing her long brown hair off her face. It was midday, the sun was hot, and they both looked remarkably fresh for having just ended a bike ride, even a short one.

"No, not really," I said, after I'd thought a minute. "I've heard of some lighthouse ghosts, though."

They shook their heads.

"We came on a motorcycle from Massachusetts. We're from East Longmeadow, out near Springfield," said Dave. He was lean and tall, with short curly brown hair. He wore a red biking shirt, and had seated himself comfortably on the grass as we spoke.

"We didn't want to pay for an expensive hotel, so we slept on the beach last night, in our sleeping bags," Holly ventured, looking at me with a tentative smile.

I smiled back. Sleeping on the beach on Block Island is illegal, but no harm had been done, and here were two people with a ghost story.

"Go on," I encouraged them.

"We probably totally weren't supposed to be doing that," she hedged, then continued, "It was somewhere on the west side of the Island, because the sun rises in the east, and that isn't where we were. It wasn't a really pretty part of the beach, not where people would usually go. It was very rocky."

"Was it near a lighthouse?" I asked, thinking how many rocky patches of beach there are on Block Island's perimeter.

"No," said Dave. He seemed sure on that point.

"Then what was that flashing green light?" Holly asked him.

I told them, "It sounds like the Southeast Light. Did you go down the stairs to the bottom of the bluffs?"

Holly shook her head. "No, we were farther down. There were

no stairs. There was a right of way to the beach, and we went down that."

Vail Beach, perhaps, I thought. South rather than west, but certainly around the corner from the sunrise. Or, perhaps one of the coves on the Island's west side.

Holly continued, "Anyway, we stretched out our sleeping bags, and we had our water bottle between the two of us. It was in this holder" — as she spoke, Dave held out the sling for my inspection — "fastened with Velcro. We drank some water from the bottle before we fell asleep, put the cap back on, fastened the Velcro and kept it between us."

"When I woke up," said Dave, "the water bottle was open, and it was out of the sling. It had been thrown about four feet away from our sleeping bags."

"And the sling was still where we'd left it, between the bags, with the Velcro *closed*," said Holly. "If someone, or some animal, had come along and taken the bottle from between us, I would have known. I'm a light sleeper. And if anyone or anything had ripped open the Velcro on the pouch, we both would have heard it and jumped up! There's just no logical way the bottle could have come out of the pouch and been thrown that far from us, with the pouch staying where it was!"

She shook her head, adding, "We saw your book in one of the stores in town yesterday afternoon, and we were looking at it before we biked around the Island.

"When we woke up this morning and saw that open bottle, out of the pouch, with the Velcro still closed — we got a *very* strange feeling. It r-e-a-l-l-y freaked us out!"

"Maybe you conjured the ghost by looking at the ghost book," I joked.

They both smiled. "It was very weird. There's no way it really could have happened," said Dave.

"So, that was why we were wondering if you've ever heard of a beach ghost," Holly concluded.

I hadn't, but perhaps now I have. Could the ghost of the beaches be someone who met an untimely death on or near the Island's perimeter, and who is now warning people against sleeping there?

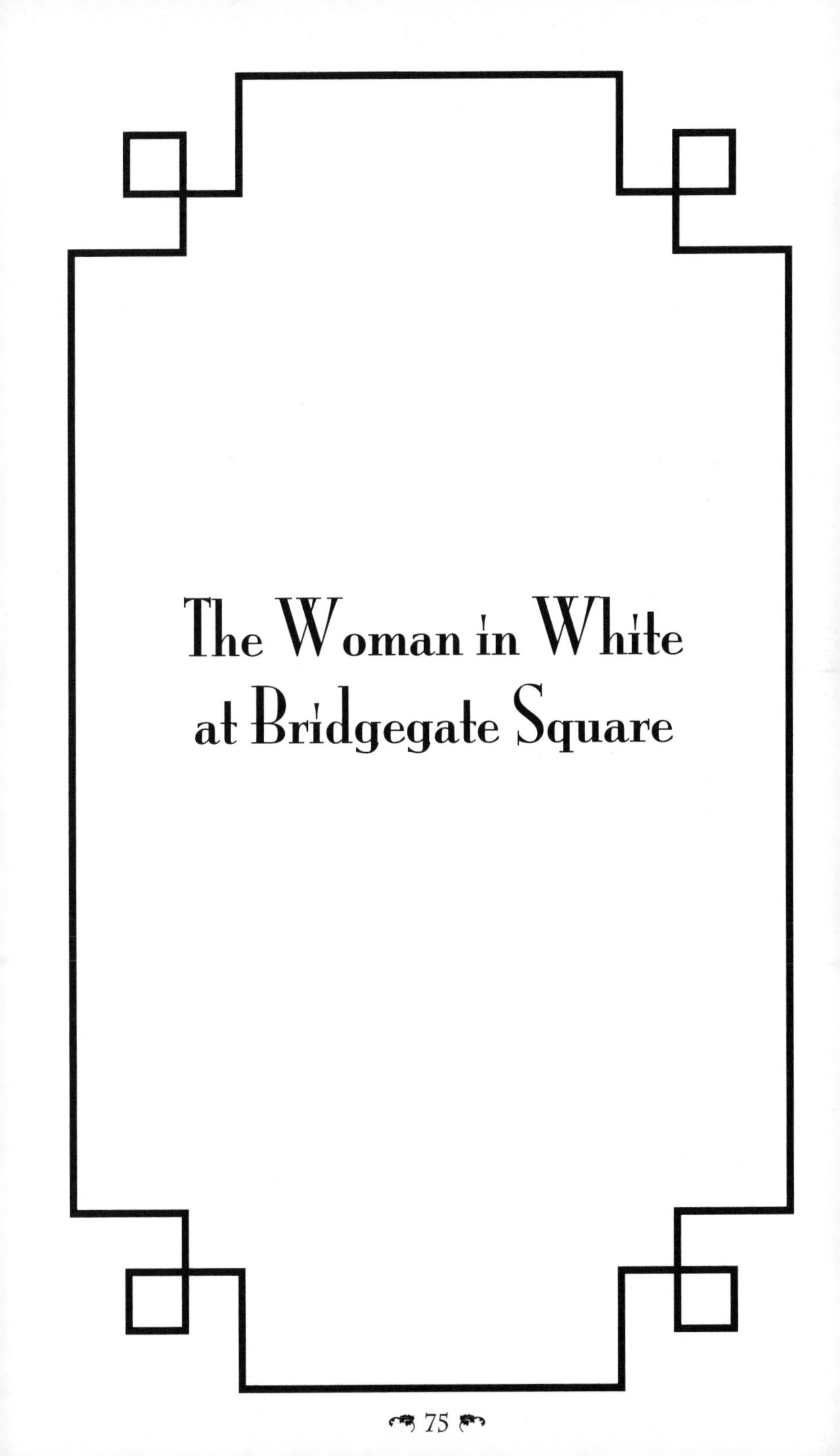

# The Woman in White at Bridgegate Square

THE NORTHWEST CORNER OF BRIDGEGATE SQUARE — comprising Washington Trust Bank, the Block Island Grocery, the Block Island Times office, Ballard Hall Real Estate and the Old Post Office Bagel Shop — was built on a filled-in wetland. New land was created there in 1932, when Old Harbor was dredged and the resulting sludge of sand and water pumped through pipes to fill in the southern reaches of Harbor Pond. Whether the one-time presence of the pond's winding waterways near Bridgegate has anything to do with the following story is unknown, but it remains a possibility, even though the events detailed here happened well after 1932.

The story was told to me in November 2008 by Melanie Carr, an employee of the Block Island branch of Washington Trust for five years. Melanie is a straightforward, logical person, not given to bouts of dreaminess or fantasies of the unreal. Her account is therefore all the more interesting:

"I used to live in the apartment above the bank," Melanie said, referring to the four-room apartment built for bank employees on the second floor of the bank office. The living quarters were added when the space formerly occupied by the Island post office was remodeled into quarters now occupied by the real estate office and the bagel shop. In the wake of a severe winter nor'easter in the 1990s that blew the roof off the post office at that location, the U.S. government took the opportunity to relocate the post office, in 1997, to a new building with greatly expanded facilities at the other end of town, next to the Harbor Baptist Church.

Melanie went on with her story, "I was in bed, asleep one night, and I woke up. It wasn't a normal kind of waking up in the middle of the night — it was as if someone or something had woken me abruptly. It just didn't feel normal, and that was one reason I got up, to try and figure out what it was. I went to the bathroom, which adjoins my bedroom. Then I opened my bedroom door to hear what was going on. I went into the hallway.

"I was the only person living in the apartment at the time. The hallway has doors to four bedrooms, with two bedroom doors on each side of the hall. The other three bedrooms were all empty.

"My bedroom is the last in the hallway. To the left of my bedroom door, in the hallway, is a door that's kept locked at all times. It leads to the apartment above the Block Island Times office, which is a separate living space entirely. I went to that door to listen — I thought maybe there was noise in there that might have woken me up. One of the previous tenants had parties in there all the time!

"There was nothing going on behind the door. Everything was quiet.

"I turned to go back to my room — and when I turned to the right, I saw a woman in a white dress in the hallway. She was *floating* away from me. I don't know how else to describe it. She wasn't walking like a regular person, she was — floating. I didn't know where she came from, and I still don't."

Did the woman in the white dress come out of Melanie's bedroom while Melanie was listening at the locked door in the hallway, then float away from her, down the hall? Or did the woman come through the locked door, and somehow float past Melanie without her knowledge? Or did she simply materialize in the hallway and start floating away from where Melanie stood?

Melanie wasn't sticking around to find out: "I immediately *ran* to the door and got out of there, fast! I didn't know what else to do, and my instinct was to get out. I stayed with my fiancé that night. I didn't want to be in that apartment alone again.

"I'd locked the door of the apartment behind me when I left, and when I came to work at the bank the next morning, there was a to-do getting back in. I didn't have the keys, it was a push-button lock, and nobody else could find any keys either, for the longest time. Eventually we got back in.

"I collected my things, and I haven't stayed in there since that night."

Melanie paused, and continued reflectively, "Someone told me that in 1945, two little kids drowned near the Beach Avenue bridge, that goes over Harbor Pond.

"And that's all I know. Maybe the woman in white was connected with that, maybe not."

The Beach Avenue bridge is located north of the bank, by way of Corn Neck Road. The bridge, from which children used to jump into the water until very recently when a prohibition was posted, is near the junction of Beach Avenue and Corn Neck Road, across from the beach.

I called Willis Dodge, who has lived here all his life except when he was in the service. Willis knew everyone on the Island during his growing-up years and later his working years, and has a great memory. Block Island is in Willis's blood — his roots go back to Trustrum

Dodge, one of the 16 Massachusetts settlers who came to the Island in 1661.

"I need to tap into your memory," I told him, when he answered the phone with a cheery "Good morning!"

"Uh oh," he responded good-humoredly. "Nobody ever said I had one."

I asked him if two children had drowned at the Beach Avenue bridge in 1945.

"They were fishing," he said immediately. "One was the little Decker girl, and the other was the Murphy boy. He was Jack Murphy's brother —Jack used to be a pal of mine. He's gone now, too.

"The two kids were found tangled together in their fishing lines. They couldn't have been more than six or seven.

"The Deckers," he added, "used to run the Weather Bureau."

After a moment, Willis said, "One other person died there about that same spot. It was Ansel Ball. He fell in and drowned. He owned Cottage Farm. I don't know how old he was. It was before my time and I used to hear my parents talking about it when I was a kid."

A call to Martha Ball revealed that her "Uncle Ansel," Hiram Ansel Ball, owned the large white farmhouse and adjoining acreage of Cottage Farm in the 1920s. The house, built by A.D. Mitchell in 1889, is referred to as the Hiram Ansel Ball House in *Historic and Architectural Resources of Block Island, Rhode Island*, with the observation, "While the house follows a traditional island form, its stylish detail surely accounts for its description in 1889 as 'a modified Queen Anne type.'"

Said Martha helpfully, "I have a picture of Uncle Ansel with his collie, Bismarck, at Cottage Farm. The year 1925 is written on the back; Uncle Ansel died in 1926. But I never heard about any drowning. He was married to Cordelia Lewis, the sister of Alice Lewis, who was my great-grandmother. Cordelia died in 1944.

"Uncle Ansel was the son of Hiram D. Ball. Hiram was the first keeper of the current North Light, and the brother of Nicholas Ball. Hiram had the old farmhouse behind Cottage Farm. He died in 1891, at the age of 73."

The "current" North Light, now standing at Sandy Point, was built in 1867 and is the fourth North Lighthouse to be built there. The first three, all built either too close to the end of the point or too far into the sand dunes, were destroyed. Hiram D. Ball's term of office as keeper, from 1861 to 1891, bridged the transition from the third lighthouse, built in 1857 and demolished in 1867, to the building of the present North Light.

Another call to Willis Dodge confirmed that there was only one Ansel Ball, and it was Martha's Uncle Ansel. "Yep, married to Cordelia," Willis affirmed.

The monument that marks Ansel and Cordelia's grave is prominent, a tall obelisk at the top of the hill in the Island Cemetery, just to the right of the road.

Another bit of information imparted by Martha Ball was that the mother of the little girl who drowned was Henrietta Decker. Suddenly, we were talking about people I knew.

I called Martha Decker Agricola, at home with her husband, Bob, on Florida's west coast for the winter. "The little girl who drowned in Harbor Pond in 1945 was my sister, Jane," she told me quietly, adding that she didn't mind talking about it or having the incident written about. "She was five at the time, and I was six. I have a brother, too; William is one and a half years older than I, so he would have been seven and a half. Jane's name was never mentioned again after her death.

"My father, James Decker, was the meteorologist at the Weather Bureau for about seven and a half years, starting when I was in first grade, in 1944. He left the position in 1952."

Years later, and many years after James Decker had died at the age of 62, Henrietta Decker became the close friend and companion of Jack Gray, a real estate broker and at one time First Warden of the Town of New Shoreham.

"Jack gave the Town, in exchange for one dollar, the land on the Neck where the Transfer Station is," Martha noted, "and he gave Esta's Park to the town, in memory of his wife, Esta." Jack and Esta had owned Esta's Gift Shop, across Water Street from what is now Esta's Park, in the space now occupied by Wave.

Jack was also an early supporter of fundraising for construction of the Island's Medical Center, and successfully got other people involved. In his honor, Edith Blane, the Town's First Warden during much of the 1980s, led the effort to erect the Jack Gray flagpole that stands in front of the facility.

Jack Gray and Henrietta Decker both died in 1988, within a week of each other. The dates given for Jack Gray at the base of the flagpole at the Medical Center are 1912-1988.

Martha Decker Agricola added, in a lighter vein, "I would have loved to see the plans for the newly renovated Weather Bureau, but that wasn't possible. My daughter Kim got married on the roof of the Weather Bureau in 1994 — she had her choice of our house on the Neck, our house on Mohegan Trail that used to be Jack Gray's house, or the Weather Bureau roof. She chose the Weather Bureau, and thank goodness the weather was perfect that day! Ed McGovern officiated at the wedding."

Of the little Murphy boy who drowned with her sister, Jane, Martha said, "I think I heard that his father died in World War II. His parents lived in the bungalow that used to stand behind the Hygeia."

Then I realized: Charlotte Murphy. Charlotte, who had always seemed so alone, whose husband and children I had never known, and who died in 1991. I called Charlotte's brother, Al Starr, whom I have known for years.

"Yes, it was my nephew who drowned, unfortunately," he told me, in a voice that was suddenly heavy. "His name was Charles Dennis. He and the little girl from next door in the Weather Bureau were fishing in Harbor Pond when it happened.

"His father, my brother-in-law John Murphy, was an aerial gunner and was shot down over Germany. My sister Charlotte raised the two boys, Jack and Denny.

"I was still in Africa when Denny drowned. It was just after the war."

I called Josephine Dugan, Al's sister. She told me, "Denny was four and a half, and his brother Jack was about six. Denny was the nicest little boy imaginable, with a freckled face, very polite. You couldn't have asked for a child with a nicer disposition."

She added, "All the children had gone to the beach that day with Henrietta Decker and my mother. Denny and Janie knew there were fishing lines in the back of the car. Without asking anybody, they went to the car, got the string lines, and decided to go fishing off the Beach Avenue bridge. Nobody realized it.

"When the adults couldn't find the children, they alerted everyone on the beach. *Everyone* was searching. It was Bill Phelan who found them, with their fishing lines tangled together."

Josephine paused. "I never told Al this," she said, "but when I was about ten, I went swimming in Harbor Pond under that bridge. I had wading slippers on, and as I swam under the bridge, one slipped off. I didn't dare go after it — the water was very deep, surprisingly deep. It was high tide, and there was very little space between the water and the concrete work under the bridge. It was awfully dark and lonely, and I was afraid to stay there. All I wanted to do was get away."

Josephine continued, "Charlotte's other son, Jack, died at the age of 41 in a car accident in Providence. That was in 1981. When Charlotte died, I arranged for her to be buried in our family plot — the Champlin plot in the cemetery — between her two boys."

Charlotte Murphy died at the age of 77, having outlived her husband and both her boys. Her older son, John Starr Murphy, served in the Navy in Vietnam, and died ten years before his mother. Little Jane Decker is also commemorated in the cemetery:

JANE WHITE DECKER
MARCH 17, 1940-AUGUST 13, 1945

Cemetery records indicate that James and Henrietta Decker are buried nearby, in the plot that they purchased in 1945.

It was all so very, very sad. I felt as though I'd clomped, heavy-footed, through the memories of the survivors of these events, people I'd known for years. Those whom I had asked, whose memories I had stirred, were incredibly gracious at the intrusion and were willing to speak with me.

All the people with whom I spoke told me that the drowning of the two children was the reason that many Island people, in more recent years, have been so upset and worried by the sight of children jumping off the Beach Avenue bridge in summer. Accidents can happen.

For readers or hearers of this story who may want to draw a connection between the ghost in the apartment above the bank and the deaths by drowning down the road in Harbor Pond, one could suggest that the woman in white might be a bereft mother or other relative or spirit, looking for lost children; or a wife seeking her drowned husband. That is conjecture. The floating apparition in the white dress could equally well be a different spirit, on the premises for some other reason that keeps her roaming in our material world, searching for a lost one, or for some sort of completion, some sort of peace.

Or — perhaps it was not simply by chance that someone told Melanie Carr about the two children who drowned in Harbor Pond. Perhaps it was a message sent to the living by a guiding spirit.

# A Coastie Ghost Update

"I HAVE A GHOST UPDATE on the Coast Guard Station," said Building Official Marc Tillson with a near- conspiratorial smile.

I'd gone into Marc's office at Town Hall to ask him about roofing materials, for an article I was writing for the *Block Island Times* House & Garden Supplement, Spring Edition. That was on March 5, 2007, before Marc and his fellow Town workers moved to their grand digs in the new Town Hall. Back then, he still had his office in one of two very long-term temporary trailers that everyone was convinced would sit in front of the Town Hall forever.

I flipped to a blank page of my little reporting notebook. "Go ahead," I told him. Marc had given me some anecdotes for my first book that had been combined into "The Coast Guard Ghost."

"This was in late September, on a beautiful Saturday," he began. "It was during the day — bright, sunny, warm, perfect fall day — and I'd been down in the basement doing laundry."

For some years, Marc has lived in the apartment that he built himself, on the first floor of the old Coast Guard Station. The station, built in 1935, is now owned by the Town. During the summer, rooms in the main building are rented to seasonal Town employees. In the off-season, Marc is the sole occupant.

Marc continued, "As I went upstairs with the laundry basket, I heard three ship's bells, as clear as could be. There's nothing else that makes that particular sound. Problem was, there was *nothing* in that building that would make that noise. *Nothing* — no clocks, no bells, no electronic devices.

"Sometimes, when old timers from the Coast Guard come out in the summer to visit the station, they ask me about the brass bells and barometers that used to be there, but those things are all gone now. It's no longer an active station, as you know.

"So that was one incident — the three ship's bells, in a building where there are no ship's bells or any other kind, either.

"The other incident happened after June Regan, the police dispatcher, had been living in the building, in one of the upstairs rooms, during the summer. She'd moved out for the winter, and left her TV sitting in the room she'd occupied.

"I was downstairs in my first-floor apartment, watching the play-offs between the Patriots and the Seahawks. At one point, I got up and went to the kitchen to get something from the refrigerator.

"It was then that I heard a man's voice, speaking in English, from the building's tower. I've heard footsteps on those tower stairs for years, as I've told you before, and the sound of men's voices, carrying on conversations in a low rumble overhead, from the direction of the tower. The footsteps and the rumble of men's voices have been heard at all seasons, in all kinds of weather, when other people have been in house, and when they haven't been.

"This time, nobody else was on the premises. I walked upstairs, and heard, of all things, the ball game score. June's TV was on, in that upstairs bedroom, playing to an empty room.

"How? There was no one there — no one!"

Marc is a man with a ready smile and an upbeat, sunny disposition, not given to gloom or moods or daydreaming. He is a person of action and deals strictly in facts and tangibles: bricks, mortar, boards, measurements, building code regulations. It is therefore ironic that he sees and hears so many mysterious, unexplainable phenomena at the Coast Guard station. Perhaps the ghosts have a sense of humor, and are playfully tweaking their host's reality base. As Marc told me three years ago, he finds these phenomena interesting facets of life in the old station.

Some might consider him a "sensitive," a person peculiarly receptive to manifestations of the spirit world. Be that as it may, Marc shrugs and says, "I don't believe in ghosts, I never have. I've just always ignored the noises, and gone back to sleep, or back to whatever I was doing."

# That Cottage Ghost Stopped This Knitter

IRIS MACAULAY LEWIS, 103 YEARS OF AGE as I write this, is a friend who lived for years on Block Island and now resides with her daughter in South Windsor, Connecticut. When I sent her a copy of my previous book in December 2005, Iris wrote to tell me the story of a ghost she had experienced on Block Island years ago, when she was staying in a cottage on Center Road.

"The Scottish side of me has a tendency to be 'fey,' which I resist because I live alone," began Iris's craggily written note. After this declaration, Iris continued:

"In the 1950s, I used to stay in a cottage on Center Road, which belonged to Louise Mitchell. I often felt I was not alone in the cottage, but was not scared as I felt it was Millard Mitchell. If so, he was playful but irritating, once taking one of my big metal #8 knitting needles away."

The only Millard Mitchell of whom I can find any record or information is Millard F. Mitchell. He is referenced in the "45th Annual Report of the Commissioners of Inland Fisheries," made to the Rhode Island General Assembly in 1915, as a Block Island fisherman holding license #60. Island Cemetery records indicate that Millard Fillmore Mitchell was a veteran of World War I. It is probable that he died in 1958, as his cemetery plot was purchased by Louise Mitchell on May 3 of that year. Members of the Mitchell clan now living on Block Island have no recollection of him.

Iris's narrative went on: "It was a bright day and I had not moved out of my chair near the window. As usual, I was knitting — you know I've always knitted, I like to keep my hands busy.

"The phone rang. When I picked up the phone, I put my knitting on the table beside me. I finished with the call and picked up the knitting, just where I'd left it. It had been practically under my nose, on the table.

"The needle was gone — forever! I had come to the end of a row.

"Joan Scott, a boarder, and I looked every place in the cottage for that needle, but it was never returned. It was a small cottage and a large needle, and we would have found it if it had been on the premises. It wasn't under my chair, or in the chair, or on the floor, it wasn't any place in the cottage! I was annoyed because I did not have another #8 needle.

"Nobody was there to take it away. I would have seen or heard a real person who came that close to me. But there was no one, and it simply disappeared.

"Other things disappeared, but might have been taken normally," Iris's note concluded.

Iris Lewis is a woman of great determination, and no nonsense. If something is missing and she can't find it, it is gone, and if she says she knows the difference between normal and abnormal taking of her possessions, then she certainly does.

Orphaned at age three, Iris Macaulay was of Indo-European ancestry and had a tumultuous, often difficult childhood that shaped a determined character. She was sent alone across the Atlantic in 1911, when she was six, and brought up by relatives in Wales and England. Some of those years were difficult and unhappy ones, but she was sent to good schools and was well educated. She trained as a Montessori teacher in a Yorkshire college in the 1920s, and upon graduation emigrated to America, arriving alone in New York at age 22.

Throughout her life, in and around two marriages and the upbringing of her three children — much of the time as a single, working parent — Iris continued to use her Montessori skills. While living in Connecticut, she was an instructor at Southbury Training School and was asked to start the first class for handicapped children in the state at Harkness, near New London. Another project, at Southbury, was taking charge of the weaving room, with 18 complicated looms. Her students adored her, and she them — Iris has loved children all her life.

Iris's last name is a married name. She is unrelated to the Lewis family that has been on Block Island for generations at Southwest Point; Iris first came to the Island in the 1950s.

Block Island had been part of Iris's varied life for over 40 years, by the time I got to know her. Iris told me, "I started coming to Block Island in 1950, and looked forward to every weekend or summer that I could spend here. I came in a weird little boat, I think it was formerly a tugboat. I was looking for a 'secret getaway,' a place where I could come to renew my spirit and soul. Friends who had sailed out here told me that they liked to go skinny-dipping in the coves at Block Island, because it was so private, even deserted. I decided that it sounded like my kind of place.

"From the first, I was totally entranced with it. I stayed in that cottage on Center Road that belonged to Louise Mitchell, and walked all over the Island, including the perimeter. Over a period of some years, I explored the Island entirely, from north to south, east to west, and could go anywhere I liked. There were no "No Trespassing" or

"Private" signs — just some of the old houses, open fields, and narrow dirt roads. There were almost no trees here at the time, except for two chestnut trees on Old Town Road."

For much of her life on Block Island, Iris lived in an apartment at E. Searles Ball housing on West Side Road. She said, of the peace and happiness she found on the Island, "I am content to get up in the morning, look out of my window and see the Great Salt Pond, whether it's misted over or clear. I like to see what birds are flying around. I enjoy looking across the pond at night, for the North Light to turn on. This is the best time of my life: I had a difficult childhood, but now I'm able to appreciate and enjoy my life. To think that I will be able to spend it all right here is the most satisfying thing I can think of."

A few years ago, realizing that she needed more care than could be obtained on the island that had always renewed her spirit, Iris moved to the mainland to be near her family. It was a difficult decision, but she knew it was the logical one.

Well into her 90s, Iris was an active knitter, a Care Wear volunteer. At her West Side Road apartment she knitted, constantly and rapidly, the tiniest baby clothes imaginable, sending them to hospitals all over the country for premature babies. She never reported any missing knitting needles there, although the ones she used for those garments were much smaller than the large #8 taken by the ghost at Louise Mitchell's cottage.

Despite Iris's admission that her Scottish side has a "tendency to be fey," she has always dedicated herself to activity, logic, learning, people, and useful work. A lover of art, jazz, classical music, non-fiction books, a tutor of languages, a traveler who backpacked through Mexico alone after her children were grown, a ruthlessly competitive Scrabble player, and a photographer at age 89 whose work was chosen for the Scenic Rhode Island Calendar, Iris has lived a full life. While on-Island, she dressed in bright scarves and jackets, adorned her jaunty hats with bits of jewelry, and loved new adventures. At the age of 100, she was taken iceboating for the first time in her life by local ice boater Charlie Gale, and enjoyed it immensely.

A waster of nothing, Iris routinely rejects idle dreams as useless wasters of her time. So, if Iris says a large knitting needle was "taken abnormally" from her cottage and never brought back, whether by the playful ghost of Millard Mitchell or some other supernatural being, she is telling the truth.

The current owners of the house and cottage on Center Road have been close friends of Iris's for many years. They report no ghostly sightings or experiences on the premises.

# The Drums and Songs of Forgotten Ancestors

"THE NAME OF THE GHOST WASN'T ARGYLE," said Charles Beck, as he settled himself in a chair in the office at the Block Island Boat Basin one afternoon during the summer of 2008. Charles is a tall bearded man, careful of speech and action, a comfortable person to talk with. I'm always happy to have a visit from him.

He was referring to the red-eyed apparition that had frightened more than one person at the house now known as Lynn's Way on Sands Pond Road, detailed in my previous book, *Ghosts of Block Island.* Charles, nicknamed Corky as a youngster, is the youngest son of the late Jean Beck, who owned the old Sands farmhouse from 1957 until her death in 1968. When Jean's estate was split among her five children, each child chose a house lot on Jean's acreage and the old farmhouse was taken over by Jean's older son, John Beck. During the four decades of Beck family ownership, the farmhouse was known to Island people as the Beck House, or Beck Farm.

"Rally told me it was Argyle," I told Charles, who had lived in Alaska, then New Mexico, for a number of years and had been at times difficult to reach. Charles shook his head gently, then gave me fuller details of the red-eyed spirit that had paid him regular visits during the years he lived in the Beck House.

"The red-eyed being was called Xenon or Zenon," he told me gravely. Xenon is an ancient Greek name that means "stranger" or "foreigner," and Zenon is the Polish form of the name. Charles had the impression at the time that the name and perhaps its owner were of Czech or Slovakian origin.

He continued, "Zenon appeared to me for many years during the time I was 10 to 20 years old. He seemed like an old man, and he had the red eyes that other people have mentioned, and seemed very depressive, or perhaps somber. He was searching for something, but didn't know where to go. He appeared to me over the years as I was trying to sleep, and he told me his name when I was 19 or 20. He left me with the impression that he had been stranded on Block Island as a foul-weather sailor after a misfortune, and had died here shortly after arriving. Why he can't move on, I don't know. He seems confused and displaced."

During the years that Charles Beck was growing up, he slept in the

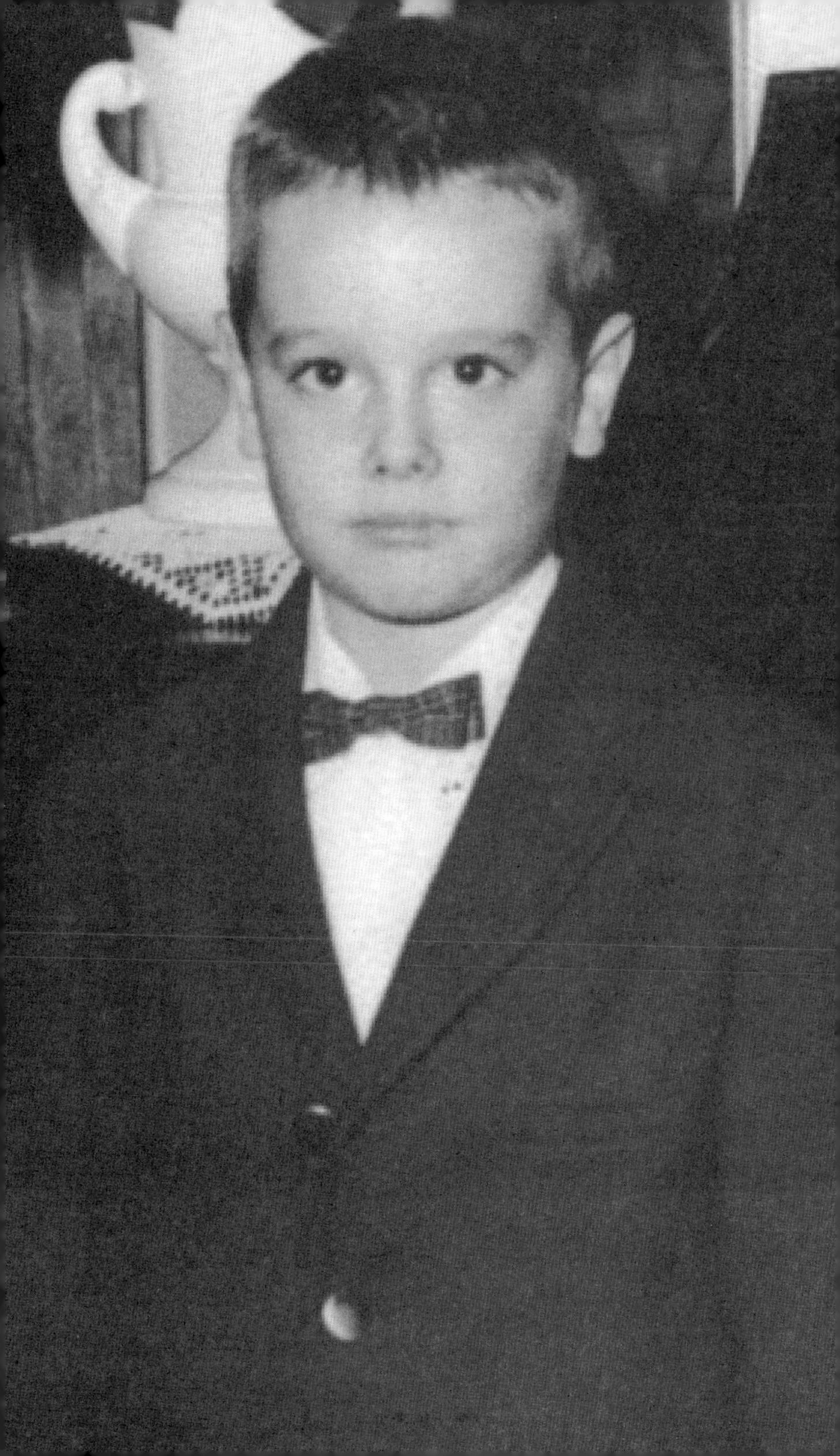

rear second-floor bedroom of his 's house. It was the oldest section of the house, built in the late 18th century. The weather-tight attic above, known as the death room, was a small, dry chamber where, in much earlier times, bodies were stored in the winter to await burial in spring, when the ground softened enough to dig. The red-eyed apparition who called himself Zenon had been seen in the attic by my husband, Rally, one morning in 1971, and the spirit seemed to originate from there, coming down periodically to visit the room below. In later years, after Charles had left Block Island, a summer tenant, Kurt Tonner, also saw the "guy with the red eyes."

Charles then told me of another experience he'd had in the house a decade later, when he was 29 or 30. He had been living in California and was visiting the family homestead with Betsy, to whom he was married at the time.

"I was staying in my 's room," he said, referring to the large front bedroom that had been occupied by his mother, Jean Beck, when she lived in the house.

"I was in a half-waking state, and I swear to you, even though I was visiting from California, I had had no drugs, no alcohol, no toxins, no chemical substances of any sort." Charles's words were a reminder that he was then, and still is, a scientifically trained psychoanalyst and psychologist, not prone to fanciful or wild leaps of imagination and not a user of chemical stimulants.

"As I lay there, in a trance-like state," he continued, "I saw five Native American elders, all males, assembling in the room. They built a fire in the middle of the floor, and throughout the evening they spoke to me in a tongue I didn't understand, often motioning me to join them. For six and a half hours they stayed; they lectured me in that strange language, very sternly, sometimes vehemently. It was a language I could not comprehend, but which I sensed was still teaching me. They made me drink a liquid from a stone cup. I had the clear understanding that they were purifying me, preparing me, blessing me.

"At four-thirty, I got up and went to the bathroom. I was ill, and vomiting. I asked Betsy to take my temperature, but I had no fever. I was exhausted, and had vivid memory of the evening's activity. In all these years, I've never forgotten the details. For weeks after that experience I felt an elation, a cleansing of perception, a broadened awareness of the world around me.

"After several years I thought very seldom of the experience. Coincidentally, I went on to do psychological work at Native American reservations in Alaska and New Mexico. I don't know whether my chosen field had a connection with that event or not — it could have.

However, I became very acculturated into the Native communities in which I lived, becoming a recognized five-feather medicine carrier of the Jicarilla Apache's Bear Society. To this day I have been blessed with a capacity to access those original five elders I met on Block Island, plus many more that I have met during my years of "rez-life," and use these skills and gifts to help heal others. It was not a path I sought — it was kind of handed to me. To this day I can invoke the songs and blessing of those five elders, and they can direct their healing intent through me to those who are receptive. I am quiet about this, in fact shy about it — I detest the thought and image of those white Wannabees running around trying to act Native. They have no concept of the power, love, mindset, and tragedy of the true Native path."

The Beck House was completely gutted and remodeled in 2003 and 2004 by its new owners, the Walsh family. The death room is there no longer, though the odd, tiny staircase that once led up to it has been preserved behind a narrow door as part of the house's history. The bedroom and an adjoining modern bathroom now have cathedral ceilings. To date, I've heard no anecdotes that indicate a continued residency by Zenon. No one else has, to my knowledge, been contacted by the five Native American elders — though as Charles pointed out, the teaching and preparation of that night appear to have been a path for which he was sought, and one that was "handed" specifically to him.

# Vapors and Rolling Rugs at the Funeral Parlor

A COUPLE CAME TO MY TABLE at one of the summer Arts and Crafts Fairs in 2006 or 2007 and introduced themselves as Russ and Rebecca Hughes. They were from Maine, and they and their family had rented and stayed in the house on Old Town Road that once housed the McAloon funeral parlor. High on a hill overlooking the north side of the road, the house is referenced in the Rhode Island Historical Preservation Commission's *Historic and Architectural Resources of Block Island, Rhode Island*: "A mansard-roof cottage with a 5-bay façade, center entrance, full-width front porch, and paired brackets on the cornices." Built in 1887, the house originally served as the Central Baptist Church Parsonage.

In those days, the Baptist church stood at the old town mercantile and political center at the junction of Old Town, Beacon Hill, and Center Roads. Says Samuel Livermore of the then-current town center, in his 1877 *History of Block Island*:

"Here the greater part of the local trading is done, at the three stores, two of which are at the four corners, and the other but a little distance north. Hither most of the sea moss is brought from the west shores, and here the West Side fishermen market their fish, and here the greater part of the poultry, butter and cheese, eggs, and much of the oil find a market. Here the town council meet and the town elections are held at the town hall. Here, too, the Baptist church is located, which can seat three hundred, leaving over one hundred of its members outside, were all to assemble there at one time. At the Center the first high school of the Island has been conducted successfully over a year."

That Baptist church burned in 1908, and some time thereafter the Baptist church and its congregation relocated to Chapel Street, at Old Harbor. The large Baptist church that once stood at the corner of Chapel Street and Weldon's Way burned in 1944.

Luckily, the Baptist church was not without resources. When Lucretia Mott Ball, the second wife of Cassius Clay Ball, died in 1941, she had bequeathed the Adrian Hotel, on a hill overlooking Old Harbor, to the Island's First Baptist Church. After the church on Chapel Street burned, the Adrian became the church's center of activity, and the present sanctuary was added in 1952.

To learn more about the original Baptist parsonage in its phase as a funeral home, I caught up with Vin McAloon at the wheel of his cab one November morning, as he waited for the ferry to arrive in Old Harbor.

"My father, Leo, was already in the funeral business out here on the Island," Vin told me. "He bought the old Baptist parsonage on Old Town Road in 1952, when the congregation needed money to relocate the church to the old Adrian.

"It took about a year for the transaction to go through, because state legislation that had allowed the land to be set aside for a parsonage had to be updated before the sale could close."

Town land evidence records reflect that the property was conveyed to V.J. McAloon & Sons, Inc., on March 10, 1953, by Lester L. Littlefield, Town Treasurer, and acting trustee for the First Baptist Church. Also acting on the church's behalf were Arthur B. Rose, Chairman of the Board of Trustees of the First Baptist Church, and Grace McLarren, the church treasurer.

Vin McAloon told me that he had owned the building for a time after his father's death, then sold it in the 1990s. Since then, it has had several owners.

The presence of ghosts in a building that once housed a funeral parlor is not surprising, though ghosts may inhabit a place for many reasons other than a building's use. When Russ Hughes told me of his family's experiences that summer, then re-confirmed them in more detail for me in December 2008, he was quite definite as to the unexplainable occurrences they had witnessed.

"My own experience occurred one evening when we were all in the living room, talking," he told me. "My mother-in-law was sitting in the chair in front of a window with a comforter.

"Outside, through the window behind her, I saw a huge rush of vapor. It collected itself for a few moments, right outside the window, then suddenly went up, and disappeared. It was very strange, and it gave me an odd feeling when I saw it. I thought it was unnatural, and it seemed at the time like an apparition. I said to my mother-in-law, 'I think I just saw a ghost behind you!'

"It was a hot summer night, and had just become dark outside. The air was still and heavy, and there was no reason for any vapor or steam to be there at all, or to be moving. There was no breeze. We checked outdoors near the window to see if there was a dryer vent or any other opening or any physical reason for steam to be there, from that building or any buildings down the hill. There was nothing. What I saw had no natural explanation, and as I said, it felt odd to me."

Russ continued, "There were three of us who had experiences with the rug in the upstairs bathroom. My wife saw it, and so did my daughter, who was 18 at the time. The rug would curl up — all by itself. That's something you just don't forget!

"My daughter also saw the bathroom door close, all by itself, while she was in the room.

"Those are the things we saw, but there was no explanation for any of them. We talked about them and we all thought the place was haunted."

There is another former funeral parlor on Ocean Avenue, just to the left of Island Hardware. It once housed the Negus funeral business, and is now a private home. While Island storytellers have told me their experiences of going through that former funeral home in years past and finding urns of cremated remains, no one has spoken of seeing ghosts there. Current owners Craig and Michele Fontaine, who also introduced themselves to me during a summer Arts and Crafts Fair, report no supernatural activity.

ROSE
ENOCH M.
1940
MARY L.
1865 — 1940

# Moonlight Became Her on Old Mill Road

An Island builder who wishes to remain anonymous told me he had some interesting ghost stories. He is a serious person, and I didn't take lightly his promise of good material.

"Don't worry," I told him. "I'll call you George." And so, George he is, and I will refer to his wife as Alice. George and I met at a local establishment one evening in the winter of 2008 and he told me his tales.

"The first ghost I ever saw," he told me, "was on Old Mill Road. My family and I were living there, in a house way back from the road, on the north side. The house is relatively new, and right behind it is the John R. Dodge Cemetery."

The house was built in 1989, I learned from the owner who built it.

George continued, "One night in May, I came home from work. It was a moonlit night, a full moon, and I pulled my car up where I had a clear view of the main house. I could see my wife standing on the front balcony upstairs. The balcony juts forth from the house, and there was moonlight behind her. Her hair was blowing in the wind.

"I shouted up to her, "Oh, you waited up for me!" I was happy to see her, and she looked beautiful in the moonlight. She turned to face me, but said nothing.

"I then remembered that our two small children were asleep in the room behind her. I apologized, in a loud whisper, for being noisy and possibly waking them.

"She still said nothing, and I went into the house. Inside, everything was quiet. I went upstairs without making any noise, went into our bedroom, and found Alice in bed. I started to say how quickly she had come back in from the outside where I'd seen her, but she was asleep. She opened her eyes, and when I said that I'd just seen her out on the balcony, she looked very confused and sleepy.

"'What? I wasn't outside at all!' she told me.

"I reconsidered what I had just seen, and realized the person outside on the balcony was Alice-like, but not Alice — a different build, different clothes. I knew that it was a human form, but realized then that it was something that didn't have a body the rest of the time.

"After that, I wasn't frightened — but when I told Alice about it, it frightened the hell out of her!

"I had no doubt, and still have no doubt whatsoever, of what I saw. There was a woman, lit by moonlight, on the balcony. She looked at me, and I was convinced it was Alice — until I went inside and found my wife asleep in bed."

George paused. "I think things tend to happen near cemeteries when there's a full moon," he said quietly, then continued:

"There was another time in that house when I had an experience that could be considered divine intervention.

"I was alone in the house with the children, quite late at night. The children were asleep upstairs, and Alice had to work late, and wasn't home yet.

"I was upstairs, and I heard footsteps downstairs, inside the house. They were very distinct, quite loud. I could hear them clearly from upstairs, and I went down to see who was there. When I got downstairs, I heard more footsteps — again, very distinct, no mistaking what they were. But there was nobody there. I looked all over the house, and there was no one, and no sign of anyone.

"I knew what I had heard, and I was quite frightened. I was worried about my children asleep upstairs, I was alone, and there were no neighbors around that time of year — all the houses on the road were dark. It was a very lonely place, and a lonely feeling. I didn't know what to do. I was afraid."

I couldn't picture George being afraid of anything. He is tall, fit, strong, and presents himself with the assurance of a person who knows nothing of fear.

George continued: "I grabbed a book from a table in the living room, not really knowing what I was doing, and opened it up. On the page in front of me, the first three words my eyes saw were, 'Be not afraid.' The book was *Crossing the Threshold of Hope*, by Pope John Paul II.

"And then, I lost all fear. I knew that whatever was in the house with me was a creature of the same God as I. I suddenly knew I had nothing to fear.

"Nothing else happened that night, no more footsteps. Nothing to fear."

George added, "I don't know if you remember a young woman named Erin O'Malley. She was a schoolteacher here, and she lived in that house at one time, sharing it with two other young teachers.

"She said that she used to wake up at two-thirty or three every morning when she was sleeping there, and would see a rocking chair in her room, rocking all by itself. The other two teachers didn't have any experiences, but Erin wanted *nothing* more to do with that house.

"My wife, Alice, had experiences at the house too, from time to time," George proffered as an afterthought. "Once, for example, she was the first one in the family to get up in the morning, and she went downstairs. On the stairs, right in the middle, there was a teddy bear, standing straight up, looking at her. She was the last one to go upstairs the night before, and she would never have left it there.

"There does seem to be a definite presence in that house," George concluded.

# Are Moonlight and Cemeteries the Key?

THE ISLAND BUILDER known in these pages as "George," who requested anonymity when he agreed to speak with me about ghosts, told me of a ghost that he saw at a house on Old Mill Road and said he had another ghost story, better even than that.

"This event took place in 2004 or 2005, I don't remember exactly which," George told me, the mid-winter evening we met for our ghost interview. "It was July 28, the anniversary of the night I met my wife, Alice, here on Block Island.

"Another person in this story is John Oettinger, my best friend. He used to live in the life-saving station at Southwest Point, and it was he who brought me here in 1988. I was 22 years old, and he told me that in the summer there was something fun going on every night, and there were loads of college girls — that's the way it was back then. It's different here now.

"Anyway, in either 2004 or 2005, we were out with our wives at Mahogany Shoals, listening to Walter McDonough. We had two cars, and when we left Mahogany, the ladies took one car, and John and I took the other. The two of us went up to the Island Cemetery to chat for awhile before going home.

"When I go to the Island Cemetery, I like to go to the top of the hill and take the second perpendicular road, then turn the car so I have a view from the top of the hill of New Harbor, Old Harbor, the water. That's where John and I were with our car.

"As we sat there, we saw a gang of kids running across the cemetery. They were shouting and laughing, and moving very fast.

"Behind them, we saw a lagger. As he got nearer, we saw it was the shape of an adolescent boy, sprinting beautifully — and he was a shade of luminescent, glowing green, all over. He was handsome, and graceful, and as he ran, he kept disappearing and reappearing, as though he was disappearing behind objects.

"We looked again, and realized that there were no obstacles, as we thought there would have been, to make him keep disappearing like that. It was as though he was running in and out of a forest of large oak trees, except there were no oaks.

"John and I both saw this green boy running, and we knew he was not a natural boy. The action of his running was too smooth — this beautiful form, running so smoothly!

"The other children, meanwhile, had disappeared — we didn't see when or where they went, they just weren't there any more — and the boy finally disappeared too.

"There is no rational explanation. There were no green lights, no illumination at all except the full moon. John and I found it difficult to believe what we had seen, but we both knew, and still know, that we saw it as I've described.

"I had seen children up in the cemetery a year before that, at about the same time of year. Again, it was a full moon. I was at the cemetery with friends, and we saw a group of kids who just seemed to appear there in the cemetery. They didn't seem to me like kids of the Island. I didn't recognize any of them, but it wasn't just that, their manner was different, they didn't seem as though they were of the Island. They didn't want to stop or talk, they hardly even noticed us, they just wanted to move on, and they went over the wall and disappeared.

"I think that there are two important elements in the stories I've told you tonight: full moons and cemeteries. At the Island Cemetery, on both of the occasions I've just mentioned, there was a full moon, and in the house on Old Mill Road where I thought I saw Alice standing on the balcony, there was a full moon with a cemetery very near.

"You should go up to the cemetery at the full moon some night. If I'm on the Island, you'll probably see me up there."

"What do you think the relationship was between the green boy and the other children?" I asked George. "Do you think they were playing a game? Or maybe they weren't aware of him?"

"As I said, he was behind them, except his running was so smooth that he didn't seem like a real lagger," George answered, "and I'm not sure the children were just regular kids, either, the way they appeared suddenly, just kept moving along, and disappeared over a wall. Why would a group of real Island kids be running around up in the cemetery so late at night?"

"Maybe," I said, "the green boy was herding them. Playing a game, but making sure they were going where he wanted them to go. Do you have any theory as to who or what he was?"

"He was unnatural," said George. "The way he moved and of course his green color. Do you have a theory?"

"A sort of Peter Pan?" I suggested. "Always youthful, leading earthly children — or their spirits — at games…"

George gave a glint of recognition. "Peter Pan," he said thoughtfully, seeming to affirm the idea. "Maybe something like that."

I thought of the entity known as the "Green Man," an archetypal figure or deity of the forest who may have derived from the god Pan. I mentioned this to George.

"Certainly, I'm familiar with the god Pan," he replied.

"I wouldn't be surprised if the green boy was somehow herding them along," I said, "and it was all a game — or like a game — to all of them."

# White Lady Rock

"YOU OUGHT TO STOP IN AND TALK WITH JANE LACHAT, one of the girls who's working for us this summer at the Book Nook," Johno Sisto alerted me with a knowing smile during the summer of 2006. "She has a ghost story about the Maze!"

Lured by a new site and a new seer, I called Jane and went to see her at the Book Nook in early September, when things were a bit less busy than in our full-throttle Block Island summer. I learned that her story went back a couple of years, but she remembered it well.

"Two summers ago, I stayed with the Laphams," she began. "I stayed with Sarah, Elise Lapham's granddaughter."

For those who may not know, Elise Lapham and her late husband, David, donated conservation easements to their property near Clay Head, which they called "Bluestone," in the early 1980s so that all could appreciate the beauty of that undeveloped landscape. David had begun creating the trail system now known as "The Maze" in the 1960s with his walk-behind mower, going from one opening to the next in stone walls that had once enclosed farmlands. The Laphams planted trees, shrubs and thousands of daffodils on their land and invited walkers to enjoy the trails even before the easement was in place. Today, the network of trails is maintained by Adrian Mitchell, of The Nature Conservancy, and his cadre of faithful volunteer trail workers.

Elise Lapham was an original member of the board of the Block Island Conservancy, and is a dedicated self-taught ornithologist and bird bander. The banding station that she established at Bluestone 40 years ago is still in operation. A bird census is taken there on a regular basis, and present-day ornithologist Kim Gaffett bands birds at Bluestone and teaches the delicate skill to others, including school students, at the site. Kim is also Executive Director of the Ocean View Foundation, and is the Town's current First Warden.

Jane continued, "In my bedroom at the Lapham house one evening, I saw a figure go by me. It was a woman in white. She glided by, and didn't seem to come from any place or go to any place — she was just there, going by me, and then she disappeared.

"I mentioned it to Sarah, and she said that others had seen the woman in white out on the trails. She told me there's a place known as 'white lady rock.'

"I saw the white lady another time, too. The second time, she was standing just outside the screen door. She was thin, with long hair, and I'd say definitely young, not old. When she moved, she glided — she didn't have legs, and didn't walk or move the way a human does.

"Last summer, I was staying at the Lapham house again. A friend was visiting me, and in the middle of the night, she woke up and then woke me up, too. 'I saw a ghost!' she told me. She was really scared.

"'Yeah, it's just the white lady,' I said, 'go back to sleep!'

"White lady rock," Jane told me, "Is up on the trails, somewhere in the middle of the Maze."

Jane was 21 when I spoke with her, and it was her third year of working on Block Island. She is an industrious young woman: in addition to the Book Nook, she had worked at the Harbor Grille and the boutique Footprints, and cleaned for Ballard Hall Real Estate. Her friend, Sarah Lapham, worked at Froozies and The Nature Conservancy. The summer of 2006 was to be Jane's final summer on Block Island; she was heading to Spain in two weeks, to take language classes and art history.

Jane was not the only person to mention "white lady rock" to me. The oddly constructed phrase was uttered by Gordon Smith one day as he and his wife, Frankie, were lunching on the Beachead porch with Robert Ellis Smith, author of the *Block Island Trivia* books; George Taber, author of *Judgment of Paris* and *To Cork or Not to Cork*; and myself. The occasion for the lunch was Bob Smith's idea that three or four Island authors get together and donate a "lunch with the authors" as an auction item to help raise money for the Block Island Historical Society at its annual Columbus Day auction. Each author donated two signed copies of his or her book to the high bidders on the auction item, and the Beachead very kindly donated the lunch we all enjoyed. We still have no idea what our presence with lunch brought at auction, and we don't need to know. We all had a great time.

Gordon and Frankie were talking about their house — on a bluff way north on the east side of Corn Neck, overlooking the ocean — and about family visiting them there.

"The last time all the children and grandchildren were here, everyone wanted to go to the Maze. They'd heard of something called 'white lady rock,' and they all wanted to go find it," said Gordon with a laugh. "They thought they were going to see a ghost, or a lady in white, or something.

"So we all trooped out into the Maze and found the place. Nothing there. But it was a very pleasant walk!"

Gordon is an engineer and has no truck with ghosts. He routinely laughs them off.

Some people see and experience ghosts, some don't. It has nothing to do with believing in them or not. Marc Tillson, over in the Coast Guard Station, admits to plenty of experiences, though he doesn't believe in ghosts.

One thing is sure: Jane Lachat saw a gliding lady in white two times, and Sarah Lapham and Jane's other friend saw her, too, on other occasions. Two years after the sighting, Jane was sticking by her story — and she wasn't the first to see the white-clad lady, either, or the coiner of the phrase "white lady rock." Others had experienced the white lady of the Maze.

# Who's at Elias's Place?

JOAN DOLAN LIVES IN ONE OF THE OLDEST HOUSES — some say the oldest — on Block Island, almost at the end of Corn Neck Road. As Joan points out, "This part of the Island was settled first." She is alluding to the first white settlers who came here from Massachusetts in 1661, landing at the north end of the Island at Cow Cove — a short distance from Joan's house.

The small, simple Cape is referred to repeatedly in town land evidence records as the "Elias Littlefield Place." Pam Littlefield Gasner, of The Block Island Historical Society, told me that the earliest date on record for the house is 1750; she added that an appraisal on record shows it as 1790. Either date could make the house the oldest on the Island to survive more or less intact; Joan Dolan believes it goes back even farther.

Elias Littlefield is shown as the house's owner on an 1850 map held by the Historical Society. Elias lived from 1813 to 1887. His wife, Nancy, also born in 1813, survived Elias by seven years, as reflected in the epitaphs collected in the transcript, *Old Cemetery at Block Island, R.I.* The cemetery transcript shows that Elias and Nancy Littlefield lost three children: Nancy, who died in 1862 at the age of one; Sands, who died in 1847 at the age of seven; and Robert, who died in 1872 at the age of seven.

A second Elias Littlefield, born in 1870, died in 1937. Whether he occupied the house for part of his life is uncertain; he may have. Historical Society records cited by Pam Gasner show John Hayes as the occupant after Elias Littlefield (and it could be Elias the elder or the younger), then Edward Hayes. Town land evidence records indicate occupancy by Edward E. Hayes in 1915, a public auction by mortgagee John B. Carpenter in 1918, and conveyance by Carpenter to absentee owner William H. Webb for $100 in 1922.

It is fitting that Joan Dolan lives in a Littlefield homestead, for she herself is a Littlefield relation.

"My ancestor was Nathanael Greene," she told me, after she had made me comfortable in a soft chair in her living room. Bambi, Joan's large orange cat, jumped off the chair to make way and seemed to take the intrusion in stride.

Joan's ancestor, Nathanael Greene, was born in Potowomut, Rhode Island in 1742. The son of a Quaker farmer who was also a blacksmith, Greene was self-educated. He ran his family's foundry and, at the age of 28, was chosen as a member of the Rhode Island General Assembly. He married a Block Island girl, Catherine ("Caty") Littlefield Greene, in 1774. Caty was born on Block Island, where her forebears had settled in the 1660s. When she and Nathanael Greene met, Caty was living at Greene Farm in East Greenwich with her aunt and uncle, Catherine Ray Greene and William Greene. It was in the "best parlor" at Greene Farm where Nathanael and Caty were married.

Less than a year after the wedding, Nathanael was called to serve in the army. He was a major general of the Continental Army in the American Revolution, rising through the ranks to become George Washington's friend, advisor, and, some said, most dependable and gifted officer.

Through her mother, Jessica Eudora Greene, Joan Dolan is related not only to the Greenes, but to the Littlefields and the Rays, the latter being among the first settlers on the Island.

I asked Joan how she first came here, and she laughed, "Oh, it had nothing to do with any of that! I came here before I was born, when my mother used to come to the Island.

"I was born in Cranston, in 1925, and as a child I always came here. My mother's best friend was named Susan Morgan, and she owned this house."

William H. Webb sold the property to Susan Morgan in 1928.

Joan continued, "Starting when I was about nine or ten, I spent every summer with Susie in this house. As soon as school was out, I'd pack my bag and take the *Lizzie Ann* out to the Island. The *Lizzie Ann* was an old sub chaser, and you could sit and drag your hand in the water.

"I loved it here! There was no electricity, no running water, and the land was all clear — you couldn't see another house for miles if you looked down the road. The closest place was Edna White's, across the road and up the hill. It's where Barbara MacDougall lives now. Susie and I used to take a bucket up to Edna's to get water from the well and bring it back here. Our light was from oil lamps, and the privy was out back.

"I had two sisters and a brother, but I was the only one in the family who really liked it here on Block Island. When I was older, I got waitressing jobs out here in the summer.

"Susie had no family of her own. She and I were close, though, and she knew how I loved it here. When I was 15, she put my name on the deed to the house. I paid her $2.00. When Susie died, it came to me."

Joan lived in Concord, Massachusetts, for a time with her husband. The couple had four children, but eventually divorced.

"That was when I moved out here," said Joan. "It was the winter of 1978, and it was cold! There was a blizzard, and the Great Salt Pond was frozen over! I moved into this house. By then, it had electricity and a furnace, but there was no insulation.

"I was able to get insulation here in the late 1980s, when the town applied for a grant to help out some of the residents on the Island with insulation and other things to make their houses more energy-efficient.

"I've always loved this house. I've painted every inch of it. I love to paint, and I'm very lucky to be here. This house has been good to me in many ways, all my life."

The contentment shows. Joan is a petite, quiet lady, a lifelong bibliophile, and has been active at St. Ann's By-the-Sea Episcopal Church for many years. With a background in nursing, she worked at Emerson Hospital in Concord, Massachusetts on the mainland and provided home care to Island residents for a time after she moved here. Befitting a churchwoman and caretaker, Joan habitually wears a smile, on a face framed by soft curls. The day of our meeting, a Wednesday, she had just had her weekly coiffure.

Asked how old the house is, Joan said, "I think it's about 300 years.

"When I came here," she added, "some of the old-timers would ask if the old still was here! Apparently there was one, once. I think it was probably in the barn, and that blew down in the 1938 hurricane.

"This used to be a farm, but Susie sold off most of the land for twenty dollars an acre — frankly, she needed the money, and nobody was that interested in land here at the time. I just have the house lot now, a couple of acres. That's all I need."

I asked Joan about her ghosts.

"They're not frightening," she said. "But they're around.

"When I moved here, I saw a lady several times, in the dining room." She indicates the room in the rear of the house, adjacent to the front living room where we are sitting.

"She was a little lady, with a full skirt and a bonnet. She moved across the dining room. I used to see her when I sat in here, reading next to the front window. I haven't seen her lately. I always thought she was someone who belonged here, and was checking me out."

Sharing the house with Joan is her son David, a photographer, who lives upstairs. "David has heard footsteps coming upstairs when he's been up there in his room," Joan told me. "When the footsteps stopped, someone knocked on the door of his room, very loudly. He said it sounded like a man, with the loud footsteps and heavy knock. But when David opened the door to answer, there was no one there."

David Dolan later told me, "I remember the knock on my door and although I really didn't think it was our ghost at the time, it is a good metaphor for other experiences I've had over the years (usually after the house was vacant for the winter and we only came in summer). I never saw the ghost but there were times when I could sense someone was there and could even tell where they were."

Continued Joan, the day I met with her at Elias's Place: "And then there's someone who knocks on the front door. That one knocks three times. When I open the door, there's nobody there. That's happened several times — and it's not the wind!"

"Maybe that's the signal they gave if someone wanted to buy whiskey from the still," I suggested. We both laughed; the explanation is as plausible as any.

I continued, "And maybe when David heard the loud footsteps up the stairs, and the knock on his bedroom door, it was the spirit of someone alerting the inhabitants of this house to a shipwreck at the north end of the Island."

That, too, is plausible. Block Island is referred to by Livermore in his *History of Block Island* as "a *stumbling-block* in the pathway of vessels." Livermore suggests facetiously that those who don't know the real origin of the Island's name might suppose it comes from this role as a "block" of marine traffic. As noted in a Rhode Island Marine Archaeology Report of 2002, nearly half of the 2,000 ships lost in southern New England in the last two centuries were lost or wrecked in Block Island's waters.

For generations, the Littlefield family was involved in lighthouse keeping and life saving. Two Littlefields were North Light keepers, Nicholas Littlefield from 1858 to 1861, and Elam Littlefield from 1891 to 1923. John Lee, married to Eileen Littlefield, was North Light keeper from 1945 to 1952.

Another famous family member, Captain Amazon N. Littlefield, rescued the crews of wrecked ships in the early years of the 20th century as a member of the Old Harbor life-saving crew.

If a ghost goes upstairs in a Littlefield house and knocks urgently on a door to find someone, it could well have something to do with saving lives after a wreck, if the ghost is, for whatever reason, caught in that particular time warp.

As for the little lady in the bonnet that Joan has seen moving through her dining room, might she be Elias Littlefield's wife, Nancy, who lost three children? Perhaps she was checking Joan out, as Joan felt she was, knowing that the new inhabitant of the house had a nursing background, and four children of her own. Maybe.

"There are noises here sometimes that you just can't put a name to," Joan says simply. "Ghosts make you feel the house is still alive. And they keep the house safe."

# The Spirit Behind the Moving Menus

HALLOWE'EN 2008 WAS THE 21ST ANNIVERSARY of Rally's and my wedding, and we celebrated with dinner at the Manisses. We were seated in our favorite dining area, the cosy one separated from the Gatsby Room by a wall of interior windows. The outside windows in the opposite wall overlook the gardens and the Abrams Animal Farm behind the hotel — though at that time of year, even at 6:00, the view was dusky and soon became dark.

We'd arrived early; Cindy Lemon had seated us and was waiting on our table. Cindy and her husband, Kim, were fairly recent year-rounders on the Island. Retired from mainland life, they had grown children elsewere and lived in a condo on High Street with their black Newfoundland. Kim worked with a local builder, and Cindy had been an organizer of the previous winter's "dinner club," a series of five fixed-price dinners hosted by Block Island Economic Development Foundation to raise money for the local community center while offering relief to an island of people bereft of restaurants in the off-season.

As Cindy went to get our drinks, dining room manager Paul Toepp came over to greet us. Paul had joined the Manisses family of employees last May, and was as always alert to familiar faces and special celebrations.

"Rally and Fran, welcome — I hear you're celebrating an anniversary," he said, beaming, then added, "I've been reading your book of ghost stories — very interesting!"

"You must have ghosts here at the Manisses," Rally challenged. "An old building like this. Maybe they just don't talk about them."

Paul became thoughtful. "You know, I had a strange experience this summer, right here in the restaurant. Cindy Lemon was with me when it happened, and she can confirm it.

"We were standing at the high, narrow bar table across from the regular bar, on the far side of the Gatsby Room." He pointed through the interior windows to the bar to indicate the spot. "It was late afternoon, just before opening time, and I had five menus standing on the bar table, propped against the support columns that go up through it.

"As Cindy and I were standing there, it was as if an unseen hand, or someone standing on the other side of the bar table, had just gone down the line and flicked each menu off the table, one after the other.

One by one, they *flew* off — they didn't just fall! It was the most amazing thing, and there was nobody there.

"It wasn't wind — there was no breeze going through, and the motion was more vigorous, like something that would be done by a hand."

Paul shook his head. "Cindy and I looked at each other, and at the menus, and I picked them up and laid them on the table. There was no explanation for them flying off the table like that, and we knew it."

At any given time, the Manisses has five menus in the house: one for cocktails, a wine list, the main dining room menu, the Gatsby Room menu, and the dessert menu. Each is encased in a substantial, fairly heavyweight cover; they are not merely sheets of paper. Rally and I had noticed the cocktail menu on the bar table as we came in, several of them in fact, propped in see-through covers against the columns for easy reading.

As Paul had been speaking, an image had come to my mind.

"Maybe it was Joan," I suggested. I was speaking of Joan Abrams, the late owner of the hotel, who had died in the spring of 2003. Joan was a vibrant, hospitable woman who raised the standard in the hospitality business on Block Island beginning in the 1960s and 1970s. I could envision her standing in the bar that afternoon with Paul and Cindy, unseen, flicking the menus off the table. But then, every time I go into the restaurant, I half-expect to see Joan there: her tall, well-clad form, her blonde hair, her ready smile and cheery greeting. She was almost always there, involved in every phase of managing the hotel and restaurant she had founded, and in which she took enormous pride. Everything had to be just right, always — and, always, she had her own prescribed way of doing everything.

Joan, her husband Justin, and their children had started visiting the Island in the 1960s, sailing their 28-foot boat from East Greenwich. After buying a run-down rooming establishment known as the Florida House in the 1960s, renovating it themselves and transforming it into The 1661 Inn, the Abrams family bought the Hotel Manisses in 1972. When they bought it, the Manisses was a boarded-up, derelict Victorian inn dating from 1876 and getting more and more decrepit from neglect. The Abrams family again worked their magic by working very hard, and restored the hotel to the grandeur of its heyday over the next several years.

Joan was well known for her abilities in decorating and design, and her interest in promoting sophisticated, first-class cuisine. Through her vision, The 1661 Inn and the Hotel Manisses became recognized as two of the finest establishments on Block Island.

Since Joan's untimely death at age 69, the businesses have been owned and operated by her husband, Justin Abrams, and their daughter and son-in-law, Rita and Steve Draper.

When I suggested to Paul that perhaps Joan had been paying them a visit that afternoon, he paused and again looked thoughtful. "Could be," he agreed. He hadn't known Joan, but must certainly, since his employment as dining room manager, have heard stories of her.

"Oh, if Joan saw something that wasn't quite the way she wanted it, she'd change it and let everyone know about it," Rally supplied helpfully. Rally goes way back with the Abrams family, to the days when they were all active in the East Greenwich Yacht Club. As he gave Paul that information, he added, "I used to bounce Rita on my knee when she was a baby!" That was almost 50 years ago.

"I know Joan never displayed the menus that way," Paul told us. "That's something I just started doing this summer."

When Cindy Lemon brought our drinks and took our dinner order, we asked her about the incident. It was, she said, as Paul had described it, seeming to be the work of an unseen hand. When we proposed to her that it might have been Joan, she considered it. She, too, had never actually known Joan Abrams.

"I've heard a lot about Joan," Cindy told us. "And her presence is always very much here, just in the way she decorated and managed, and in the way everyone remembers her. I wouldn't doubt it a bit, that she was standing on the other side of the table, or just walking by, and decided to knock the menus off."

And that is the way it will be left. The Manisses will always be Joan's place, and I'll bet she's still keeping track and making sure everything is done just so.

# Winfield's Ghost

A FAMILIAR-LOOKING COUPLE APPROACHED ME in the summer of 2007 as I sold my books at one of the Arts and Crafts Guild fairs on the lawn of the Block Island Historical Society. "We're Jon and Pam Vaccaro," they told me. "We come to the Block Island Boat Basin every summer."

Of course! The name was familiar, even though I couldn't place the faces at first. My job at the Boat Basin keeps me mostly in the office above our ship's store. While I'm familiar with many of our customers' names, from the paperwork that crosses my desk, I know relatively few of the people. That is a sad fact of working a desk job on the Island in the summer. Jon and Pam wouldn't have known who I was, either, except that they recognized my name from the book cover, and knew that my husband, Rally, runs the Boat Basin.

Jon and Pam are from Darien, Connecticut, and for years have spent summer vacations at the Block Island Boat Basin aboard their motor vessel, "Sunsational." Coincidentally, Jon's mother is a Migliaccio, related somehow to Rally.

"We've read your book," Pam said, "and we were wondering why you don't have anything in there about the Winfield's ghost."

It occurred to me that I had heard rumors, from time to time, of a ghost at Winfield's, but the rumors had never been fleshed out for me, so to speak. I told the Vaccaros that nobody had offered an account of a Winfield's ghost.

"We were there one night with a group of friends," Jon told me. "The dinner was excellent. They have a great menu and some of the best food on the Island.

"But when my salad plate was put on the table, it jumped — literally *jumped* — off my place at the table and onto the floor, and broke.

"Later," he continued, "when I took out my wallet to pay the bill, my wallet went flying in the air and all my cash and credit cards fell out!"

"*Everyone* saw it!" said Pam, her eyes wide. "We couldn't believe it — nothing like that had ever happened to us before — ever! It just wasn't a normal occurrence."

"I asked if that had ever happened to other people at Winfield's," said Jon, "and the waitress said, 'Oh, you got the ghost!'"

One evening in the summer of 2008, I went to Winfield's for an early dinner with a friend, Debbie Dalrymple. We were on our way to a jewelry show and sale at someone's house way up at the end of Corn Neck, and we ate appetizers and salads while sitting at Winfield's cozy bar. It was too early for other diners; we had the space, and bartender Gloria Hall Daubert, all to ourselves. As we were waiting for dessert, I asked Gloria about ghosts.

"Oh, there's something here, I think!" she replied, in her energetically brisk, forthright manner. "Years ago, I worked here in the winter and I never liked to go down to the basement alone. It just didn't feel right down there, and I always came up as quickly as I could. On slow nights, especially in the winter, this old building can be scary."

Gloria and her brothers and sisters have almost all worked at Winfield's, or the adjoining Yellow Kittens, at one time or another and some still do, even though all have been grown up for years and many have children of their own. Gloria comes from a family of eight — four boys and four girls — whose names all begin with "G." They grew up on Block Island, the children of Barbara and Allen Hall. Barbara, the sister of Willis Dodge, is a descendant of Trustrum Dodge, one of the group of first white settlers from Massachusetts who settled Block Island in 1661.

The Yellow Kittens was built by another Dodge, Winfield Scott Dodge, Sr., and later run by his son, Winfield Scott Dodge, Jr.

The name Winfield S. Dodge appeared in the news in 1895. That year, long before national Prohibition, the citizens of Block Island had voted that Block Island would be "dry," a place in which no alcohol would be sold. It is no coincidence that one of the Island's influential citizens at the time was Lucretia Mott Ball, 29 years of age in 1895. Descended from at least six of the Island's prominent early families, Lucretia was the second wife of Cassius Clay ("C.C.") Ball, who had inherited from his father, Nicholas Ball, the grand Ocean View Hotel, the largest on the Island. Lucretia was also the founder of the Block Island chapter of the Women's Christian Temperance Union (WCTU), and was the chapter's first and only president until her death in 1941 at the age of 74.

Some Island business owners of the Gilded Age didn't hold with prohibition, and openly sold liquor at their establishments that summer. The WCTU brought two undercover detectives to the Island to purchase liquor, and four Island people were convicted of illegal liquor sales. They received jail sentences of 10 to 30 days and fines of $10 to $60. The four were Darius Dodge, a state representative from Block Island; Aaron W. Mitchell, the local Sealer of Weights and Measures; John L. Macomber, an Island constable; and Winfield S. Dodge, keeper of the Yellow Kittens tavern and restaurant.

The attitude of many on Block Island at the time, according to a brief account in the *Newport Journal*, December 21, 1895, was that "There appeared to be no objections to the summer visitors spending all they wished for beer and other liquors," whereas in the winter, with the tourist trade gone, the local population who bought alcohol were "those least able to waste their substance on buying rum or whiskey."

The name of another Dodge family member, Richard Dodge, is associated with the Yellow Kittens. Richard is the "Dead Eye Dick" Dodge for whom Dead Eye Dick's Restaurant, in New Harbor, is named. Richard and his wife, Cecile Desmarais Dodge, owned Dead-Eye's for three decades, from 1935 to 1967. Cecile Dodge, in fact, ran three businesses: Dead Eye's, The Blue Dory Inn (which had been Dick Dodge's homestead), and the Yellow Kittens.

Police dispatcher Betty Desmarais Gann and her brother, plumber John Desmarais, are the niece and nephew of Cecile Dodge. I knew that Betty had worked for her aunt at the Blue Dory in the late 1960s, after Dick Dodge's death, so I called her to see what she knew about the Kittens.

"I worked there when it was called the Cat and Fiddle, winters only, in the early 1980s, for Diane Tripler," Betty responded. "I heard lots of tales about the place, and the basement, but I don't know anything first hand."

I had asked her, in fact, if she knew anything about Winfield Dodge. For years, I had been told that he had died in the building.

Diane Tripler, reached at home the day before Thanksgiving, was able to fill me in a bit more. In answer to my question, she said, "The story was that Winfield Dodge fell down the basement stairs and lay there until his body was found."

It should come as no surprise that the stories that get passed around don't always end up quite right, as was revealed to me later by another source.

Diane added, "Kathy Jones and Ed McGovern both worked there with me, and we all felt Winfield's presence, for sure. In the basement, we definitely felt it."

She elaborated: "The first year or so that I was running the Cat and Fiddle, there was an on-demand water heater in the basement. Quite often, a draft would blow out the pilot light, and someone had to go down with a flashlight to reset it and stay there for forty-five seconds until they were sure it was on. That was the *longest* forty-five seconds in the world! When the pilot blew out, everyone got really busy and started to move around very quickly, because nobody wanted to be the

one to have to go down and reset the heater.

"Dan Cahill was my dishwasher in those days," she concluded, adding gently, "My washing machine is running over — I have to go deal with that now."

I thanked her for her helpful information, and we rang off.

I remembered that Elwin Dodge, up on Amy Dodge Lane, had been quite informative a year ago when I'd asked him about Richard Dodge, his father's cousin.

Queried about Winfield Dodge, Elwin replied, "Well, Claire Pike is Winfield's niece, so you ought to ask her. I don't really know that much about him, to tell you the truth, except that he was a great big man, over six feet tall, and he'd get to drinking and hollering sometimes. As a kid, I was afraid of him."

"Which Winfield Dodge do you want to know about?" asked Claire Slate Pike graciously, when I called her. She proceeded to tell me about both of them.

"Winfield Scott Dodge, Sr. was my mother's dad, my grandfather, and he built the Yellow Kittens," Claire told me. "He was born in the little Cape Cod house right next to the Gables Inn. Everyone who lived on that street was a Dodge, and we were all related. That's why it was called Dodge Street. I was born in the house on the corner where Leslie Dodge Slate lives now. I'm a Dodge on my mother's side.

"Winfield Scott Dodge, Jr. was my uncle," she continued. "He ran the Yellow Kittens in later life. He was married a short time to Helene Cundall, who owned the Shamrock, which used to be the Ocean View annex."

"Did either of the Winfield Dodges die at the Yellow Kittens?" I asked her, thinking I must sound rather blunt.

"Oh, that was my uncle," Claire responded. "Grandpa died at home.

"Winfield Scott Dodge Jr., my uncle, died in the kitchen at the Yellow Kittens. He fell on the floor, and he was found there. Nobody was quite sure how long he'd been there — I think it was probably several days.

"It was so sad!" she added, with great feeling. "He was my mother's brother! It was just awful!"

Again, I had stumbled into a sad and terrible event that had affected people I know and love now, on this Island. Claire Pike said she did not mind my writing about her Uncle Winfield, and she very graciously reviewed this story before publication.

The epitaph noted in *Old Cemetery at Block Island, R.I.* by Mrs. Helen Winslow Mansfield in 1950 reads, "Winfield Scott Dodge Jr., R.I. pvt.

1 cl. 17 Coast Guard, April 6, 1942."

Claire sighed gently and shook her head. "Uncle Winfield had a drinking problem," she told me. "When his marriage to Helene ended, he took it badly and his drinking got worse. He used to live at the Kittens in those days, while he was running the place, so he was there at all hours."

And that is the only death I have heard of at the Yellow Kittens. It stands to reason that the ghost at Winfield's would be that of Winfield Dodge, Jr., who came to an untimely end on the floor of his own kitchen.

As a former owner, he has the run of the building. Perhaps it was he who created drafts to blow out the pilot light on that water heater — maybe he enjoys keeping the Winfield's and Kittens employees on their toes, and knew that they would leap into action in response to the equipment malfunction — even though their activity was designed to keep them from having to fix the problem. Or perhaps Winfield Scott Dodge, Jr., thinks the wonderful, innovative cuisine at Winfield's is too fancy these days, and makes his thoughts known by pulling salad plates off the table and dropping them on the floor. Perhaps, in a playful moment, he likes to "tweak" everyone by lifting a wallet in the air and pulling out its contents, just to get people's attention. Perhaps.

# Welcome, Welcome Dodge

KAY MCMANUS GAVE ME A HUGE SMILE and a warm welcome as she answered my knock at the front door of her Spring Street house. It was fitting, not only because Kay is a welcoming person by nature, but because her farmhouse is the Welcome Dodge House, built by Welcome Dodge, Jr. in 1868, when he was 23 years old. His father, Welcome Dodge Sr., lived with his wife, Cornelia Ann, just up the hill in the house on Amy Dodge Lane now owned by Dan and Rosemary Millea.

"This house was between a post and beam construction and a balloon frame," said Kay, of her own house. An architect, Kay renovated the Welcome Dodge House to make it more practical and livable for this century even as she preserved and incorporated the old structure and finish work.

"Welcome Dodge was a farmer and a fisherman," she told me as we settled comfortably, with cups of freshly made green tea, in the north "view" room, with its vista of Old Harbor and the northeast end of the Island. There are two easy chairs facing the view, and a desk with a computer behind the chairs, against the wall. The professional owner of the house can enjoy the view at all times, whether she's working or relaxing. The morning we sat there, December 3, 2008, was clear and sunny; past the sweep of green pasture that is now the house's front yard, the water sparkled in front of us all the way north.

Kay added, "Sherman and Welcome Dodge used to wash their fishing nets together in the spillway between this property and St. Andrew Parish Center." She pointed to the far end of the lawn, where a natural swale, host to phragmites, marks the dip in the land as it transitions to the church property.

"Dub Barrows grew up in this house," she added of a mutual friend, born on Block Island, who now lives on Old Town Road. "He came up here to visit me a few times, and told me that when he was growing up here, his family used to rent rooms. There were five bedrooms upstairs in those days, and when they had guests, Dub slept downstairs. His bedroom, when there were boarders, was the little southwest corner room in the rear of the downstairs. The room behind us used to be two rooms; it's been enlarged to include that rear corner bedroom. When you come in the front door, there's a front bedroom off to the right, and that's always been there.

# ABSTRACT OF THE TITLE

## OF

## Welcome Dodge Jr.

— AND —

## Witman W. Littlefield

To a farm on Block Island
Rhode Island at the "South
East" part of the old Capt.
James Sands "Great Lots"

"Dr. Dunn, the previous owner, changed the upstairs from five bedrooms to three and a bath."

Kay added, "Originally, there was another door on the south side of the house, for the family to use. The front door, here on the north side, has always been there, though I thought that in the old days, a front door was never put on a northern exposure."

Dub Barrows — whose real name is the beautifully poetic sounding Silas Littlefield Barrows — later told us that the front door was placed on the house's north side to accommodate boarders, even though conventional wisdom might seem to dictate that a north-facing front door would be impractical in winter, in the face of cold nor'easters. Dub explained that people who took in boarders always placed the front door of the house at the bottom of the staircase, near the dining room, so the boarders could come downstairs, take their meals, then leave the house without having to go through the kitchen and other "working rooms" at the back of the house. The "view room," where Kay and I sat during my visit, was to the right as one descended the stairs, and had been used as a dining room by Dub's family.

Dub added that the privy used to stand in a northeast spot, out in the yard, so the boarders could easily walk to it from the front door as necessary.

Boarders were a summer event; in the winter, a northern front door could be kept closed against the cold and the snow that would drift and pile against it with the wind. The south door, in the lea and the sun and nearer the barn, would be a more practical access for family and workers at any season, but especially in winter. There was also a door on the east side of the house, Dub told me.

"Where was the south door? Between those two windows?" I asked Kay during my visit, indicating the living room behind us.

"That's what I used to think," Kay replied. "It seems like a natural place for it. But when I began renovating, I saw that the door used to be off to the left. It opened into that little hallway. The hallway used to be a mudroom."

The little hallway that was once a mudroom connects the kitchen with the rear room that is now used as a living room. Off the hallway, opposite the wall where the south door used to be, is a half bath.

The Welcome Dodge property, Dub Barrows told me when I called him for additional reference, was a small farm, about 21 acres. Originally it was much bigger; Dub has the first deed, and it includes records dating back to 1637, when the Massachusetts Bay Colony took the Island from Miantoromo, the chief of the Narragansett tribe.

In 1658, Massachusetts conveyed the entire Island to John Endicott,

Richard Bellingham, Daniel Dennison and William Hawthorne. In 1660, the last transfer of the entire Island took place when those four owners sold it to the company of 16 men whose ranks included the Island's first white settlers of 1661.

The deed that Dub showed me goes up to 1869. The original house on the property burned, Dub said, and it was then that the present house was built by Welcome Dodge, Jr. in 1868. The barn behind the farmhouse, separated from it by a stone wall, is now owned by abutting property owners Arlen and Audrey Lichter. The newly renovated house on the other side of St. Andrew Parish Center, formerly the home of Joe and Betty Tucker, was originally the sheep barn on Welcome Dodge's property. A little house that sits behind St. Andrew Parish Center and is now used for the church's twice-yearly "Not New Boutique" clothing sales, was built on Barrows land with Dub's father's consent as a cow barn, by the owner of the house that once stood where the Parish Center is now.

Kay McManus's land extends all the way to the water in front of her house, behind the Parish Center, and around Old Harbor Point, in front of newer houses there.

"Everything north of the wall," Dub told me, "belonged to our family. We owned the laneway to the water, and we had the seaweed rights and salvage rights. Seaweed rights were always an important thing to have." He also mentioned that the Parish Center's septic system occupies a piece of McManus's property, on the east side of the wall.

The rights enumerated by Dub run with the land, and Kay holds the laneway, seaweed and salvage rights to this day. "The way the salvage rights were explained to me," she laughed, "was that if the *Queen Mary* is wrecked in front of our property, we can claim the whole thing, but we also have to get rid of it!"

Kay had told me that Dub Barrows's mother was a Dodge. She was actually a Littlefield, Dub told me — hence his middle name — but Dub's grandmother was a Dodge. She had a most wonderful name: Bathsheba Ball Dodge Littlefield.

Dub's great-great grandmother was a Ball: Cornelia Ball Dodge and Welcome Dodge, Sr. were Dub's great-great grandparents. Dub is also related to the Sands family, and to the Rose family through the marriage of his mother's sister to Harry Rose. "I can't throw any stones on this Island," he laughed, after reeling off the names.

Kay McManus filled me in on a more recent owner of her house, Dr. Hillary Lincoln Dunn, who bought the house and property from Dub's father in 1956. "Dr. Dunn was a dentist," Kay told me. "People called him Steve. He played soprano sax with big bands to put himself

through Harvard. He was the uncle of a neighbor of my mother's on Staten Island.

"Sally Stephens first brought me to Block Island, and I was surprised to find out that an uncle of a neighbor had a home here. We stopped to visit him one day, and kept the visits up each summer."

During the time he lived on the Island, Dr. Dunn continued his musical gigs, playing at Dead Eye Dick's in the summer. The late Joan Butler told me, in 2007, "On Sunday nights, there was the Block Island Symphony at Dead Eye's with the three Bills — my husband Bill on gutbucket, Bill Hall, and Billy Stubbs, with Steve Dunn on clarinet making a fourth. It was a lot of fun."

It was Dr. Dunn who, in 1979, gave two acres of his property to St. Ann's By-the-Sea Episcopal Church, in memory of his first wife. The original St. Ann's, which once stood down the street on property now belonging to The 1661 Inn, was destroyed in the 1938 hurricane. The parish built the present-day St. Ann's church and vicarage in 1985, on the property given by Dr. Dunn.

I asked Kay about the ghosts in her historic house, for she had mentioned them to me after the publication of *Ghosts of Block Island.*

"I saw one ghost, and my daughter, Cyndi, saw at least two," she responded readily. "The ghost I saw was in the mirror in the living room."

She led the way to the room and pointed to the east wall, where an architectural study of her own now hangs. "There used to be a mirror hanging where that picture is now," Kay told me. "It was in an old wood-with-plaster frame that I found in the house when I bought it — the first Mrs. Dunn collected antiques.

"When I was in that room, near the mirror, I would look up and see an old woman in the mirror behind me, just looking at me. She was a little woman, with a small face. Her hair was tied back in a bun — it was silvery hair. She always wore black, and she always had a gray shawl on, that looked knitted or crocheted. I saw her more than once, always in the mirror, but I haven't seen her for awhile now.

"My daughter and I both saw the same woman upstairs, too." She conducted me upstairs and pointed to the end of the hallway, to the right, at the top of the stairs. "There used to be a small mirror on that wall," she said. "When we came upstairs and turned right, we would see that same woman, reflected in the mirror."

Kay led the way into the bedroom to the right of where the mirror once hung, a small northwest corner room. "This was Cyndi's room," she said. "Cyndi used to wake up at night and see that same woman rocking in the corner of the room. There was no rocking chair there, though. But she saw the woman sitting there, rocking."

At the time Kay told me this story, she thought that the ghostly lady was Cornelia Ball Dodge, the wife of Welcome Dodge, Sr. Kay's identification of her ghost was based on two charcoal drawings shown to her by Dub Barrows. "When Dub Barrows came up to visit," Kay told me, "he brought charcoal drawings of Welcome Dodge and his wife to show us. We took one look at them and immediately said, 'Those are our ghosts!' So, we know who our ghosts are!"

As Kay and I have since found out, the faces in the charcoal portraits are those of Dub's great-grandparents, Welcome Dodge, Jr. and his wife, Olive L. Dodge — not those of Welcome Dodge, Sr. and Cornelia.

In the nineteenth century, infant and childhood deaths were more common than now; medical knowledge of causes and prevention of illness and death had not evolved to its present state, nor was medical help as readily available, especially on a small rural island. The Welcome Dodge family, like others on Block Island, had lost young children. One of these was the daughter of Cornelia and Welcome Dodge, Sr., and another was the daughter of Olive and Welcome Dodge, Jr. Ten years apart in age, they bore the same name — that of Welcome Dodge, Sr.'s wife — and died within two months of each other in the same year. The epitaphs listed in *Old Cemetery at Block Island, R.I.*, copied by Mrs. Helen Winslow Mansfield in 1950, are:

CORNELIA ANN
DAUGHTER OF WELCOME AND CORNELIA ANN DODGE
DIED FEB. 24, 1866
AGED 10 YRS. 7 MOS. 11 DS.

CORNELIA ANN
DAUGHTER OF WELCOME AND OLIVE DODGE
BORN MARCH 6, 1866
DIED APRIL 12, L866

"I think," said Kay, "that the lady ghost was watching over Cyndi, waiting until Cyndi was old enough so that she knew Cyndi would be okay. Those two little girls had been lost to the family, within a very short time of each other.

"Once Cyndi turned eighteen, the ghost disappeared."

Kay added that she and Cyndi had experienced other apparitions as well: "When I was in the kitchen, I used to hear the screen door in the breezeway slam shut! There were no footsteps, but you *knew* someone had come through that door and into the kitchen.

"I think it was hired hands from the farm — they would have come in through the back door, had dinner in the kitchen, then gone upstairs to the quarters above the kitchen, where they stayed.

"Sometimes I've been in the kitchen and heard men's voices upstairs, talking. I couldn't hear what they were saying, it was just the sound of their voices. I heard them quite a few times.

"None of this has happened for several years now," she added, then continued: "There was another ghost, too, that Cyndi saw outside. It was after we mowed the field to the east of the yard in front of the house, past that break in the stone wall, between us and Old Harbor Point.

"Cyndi also saw Welcome Dodge, upstairs in the house, after we'd mowed that field. He had a long beard."

"Maybe he was here to thank you for mowing the field," I suggested.

"Maybe," said Kay, smiling.

A few days later, when Kay and I visited with Dub Barrows, he remarked that his grandmother, Bathsheba Ball Dodge Littlefield, had also lost children, three of them. He said that Kay's description of the ghost as a small woman wearing black, with her hair tied back in a bun, sounded like his grandmother, and he said he wished he had a picture of Bathsheba to show us. "I wish I could see my grandmother again," Dub told us. "I used to love to spend time with her!"

It is possible that more than one spirit watches over the Welcome Dodge House. Though Kay and Cyndi have positively identified Olive as the ghost they have seen, perhaps Cornelia Ann Ball Dodge and Bathsheba Ball Dodge Littlefield also have a share in the protective watch over children on the premises. All three of the Dodge women lost children of their own.

According to the epitaphs collected by Mrs. Helen Winslow Mansfield at the Island Cemetery in 1950, Bathsheba Ball Dodge Littlefield and her husband, Silas N. Littlefield, lost three daughters during the 1890s: Olive, at an undetermined age in the early 1890s; Hilda, at nine years old in 1904; and Thelma May, at two years old in 1899.

Dub also told me that when Welcome Dodge's sizeable property was split among his descendants, it was Bathsheba who received the house at the bend of Spring Street, now known as "Admiralty House." Bathsheba, incidentally, was given the marvelous nickname "Bashy" by her family and friends.

The day Kay and I visited Dub, he showed us the charcoal drawings of Welcome and Olive L. Dodge. Welcome is a substantial man with a smooth, rounded face and a long, full beard. Olive is a dark-haired beauty. She was four and a half months older than Welcome, according to the records, and predeceased him by six years, in 1914. Welcome Dodge, Jr. died at 75 in 1920; Olive, born in 1844, lived to 70 years of age.

Said Dub, of his great-grandmother's portrait, "My daughter sometimes looks like her." He showed us a photograph of his daughter, Carol, and indeed she does look like her great-great grandmother.

"Do you think that ghosts are always around us?" I asked Kay, the morning I visited with her at her house.

She replied, "Well, it's light — it's energy! I used to see streaks of light in the garden while I was out there. I think ghosts are a form of energy. And there are all sorts of relics, too, that I've found on the property – bits of pottery, old shoes. People didn't go to the dump back then.

"I haven't seen or heard the ghosts for several years, now," Kay added lightly, with a smile.

"Too bad," I told her. "They sound like nice ones, and they'd be good company to have around."

"Well, as I said, I think our lady ghost was watching over Cyndi," said Kay. "When she knew Cyndi would be all right, maybe she thought she didn't need to watch over her anymore."

Kay and I had agreed that I would come to her house a few days later, when her daughter Cyndi would be on the Island. I drove to the house on a sunny Saturday morning and was welcomed at the front door by Cyndi, holding baby Nathaniel in her arms. Nathaniel may be the happiest, most smiling baby in the world. He smiled when we met, smiled and laughed as we talked in Kay's kitchen. "He's always like this!" Kay and Cyndi both told me.

In the kitchen, the McManus Christmas cookie-baking tradition was in full swing. I took a chair at the kitchen table and grabbed a recipe magazine as a firm backing for my writing pages, while Cyndi relaxed a few moments from baking to tell me about her experience of ghosts in the Welcome Dodge House.

"The first time I saw a ghost was when I was fourteen," said Cyndi, now 37 years old. "It was our first year in this house, and we rented it for a summer before buying it.

"I saw the ghost in the mirror downstairs," she said, referring to the mirror in the living room where Kay had seen the face of an old woman.

"It was flashes of light at first," Cyndi recalled. "Then a year or two later, when I was fifteen or sixteen, there was a face that would linger and look at me, a woman. She was the same ghost every time, and her face was the one in the charcoal drawing that Mr. Barrows showed us. She was always on the left side of the mirror, and always observing me. It was startling, at first, to see her, but she was never threatening."

Cyndi said she had also seen Olive's ghost upstairs. "My room was always the corner bedroom upstairs, the northwest one. It's really tiny. When I was fifteen or sixteen, I used to see the lady ghost in the room almost every night. She would be sitting in the corner of the room, rocking, but there was no rocking chair in the room. I saw her whole body, sitting and rocking. She always had a shawl on, and sometimes it looked as though she was knitting, doing some kind of work with her hands."

It was as Kay had described it to me a few days before: the shawl, the rocking woman. Then Cyndi startled me by adding casually, "She was up in the air."

"Up in the air?" I said, trying to visualize. "How far?"

Cyndi held a hand up, as if gauging height. "A good four feet up in the air."

"Rocking," I said.

"Rocking," Cyndi confirmed.

"Did you ever talk to her?" I asked.

"No," Cyndi replied, "but if I saw her again, I would try to engage her in conversation.

"I've seen other ghosts here, too," she added. "I saw Welcome Dodge in an upstairs bedroom that has now become the upstairs bathroom. He was in his white nightgown, and he was grumpy looking! That was after we'd mowed the pasture.

"And there was a younger guy that I'd see — I don't know who he was. He was thinner in the face, with short hair parted to the right side. He was in a nightgown, too, and he was out in the field. I didn't see him as often as I saw Welcome.

"I used to see Welcome into my twenties, after the lady ghost had stopped visiting me. I stopped seeing her when I was eighteen."

Cyndi turned to her happy, very human and substantial baby. "Ethan is almost six years old now," she said thoughtfully, referring to her other son. "I think he may have seen something — he was telling me about a man in the breezeway one day, but then he wouldn't say anything else. He's older now, so maybe he'll see more."

Added Kay, from where she stood at the stove, "We've been wondering if the lady ghost might come back, to watch over young children in the house."

"We're not here all the time," said Cyndi, "but we'll be spending time here this summer so Ethan can start getting involved at the Block Island Club. I remember doing that when I was young, and I loved it!" Cyndi also worked on the Island during summers, she told me, from the age of 14, at the Water Street Café and Ben & Jerry's.

Cyndi, with Nathaniel in her arms, walked me to the front door. In the living room I was introduced to Ethan. Though engrossed in a TV show, Ethan stood and shook my hand when we were introduced. He then wondered aloud about the status of spoons or bowls to be licked.

"In awhile," his mother told him. "A little at a time."

SAMUEL ALLEN
Died

# The Ghost and Mrs. Lofaro

IT WAS A BLEAK MIDWINTER DAY IN DECEMBER 2008 when I visited the home of Anna and Mike Lofaro at Southwest Point. Inside, all was a-bustle. Most of the windows in the house were being replaced by Norris Pike's crew — Pat Cobb and another worker — due to constant buffeting by west winds and salt.

I held the door for a man with a newly cut board and called out to Anna, "I'm here — I followed the real workers in!"

"Here's a paint brush, get started!" rejoined Pat's voice from a small room near the front hall.

Anna was in the kitchen, as I knew she would be. She is a consummate cook of anything and everything, but today the kitchen was cool and there were no aromas of Christmas cookies baking.

Anna greeted me, as always, with an energetic smile and sparkling eyes. "We have to keep the windows open because of the polyurethane," she told me. "I can't bake anything — it'll absorb the odor of the poly while it's cooling, and taste like it too. Oh well, what can one do? Would you like a cup of tea?" she went to a shelf and started reeling off a list of flavors; we both chose Candy Cane Lane in honor of the season.

Pat Cobb appeared at the kitchen door. "We need to have a window open in here because of the fumes," he said to Anna apologetically.

"We were just thinking it's not quite cold enough in here," I commented, as Anna cranked open a window above the sink. Pat grinned and disappeared, brush in hand.

The hot peppermint tea, its flavor rounded with vanilla, was welcome and comforting. We forgot all about the polyurethane and the chill air.

"When my sister was visiting from North Carolina a few years ago, she brought a friend with her," Anna began. "That was in about 2005. The friend, Sandra, is psychic, and almost as soon as she set foot in the house, she told me, 'There's somebody else living here.'

"I told her I already knew that. During her visit here, she walked around outside a lot. She told me that the other being here was the ghost of the man who had built the stone walls and had wanted to buy this property at one time. He couldn't afford it, but he had always felt very protective of the land.

"This piece of property was once a sheep farm," Anna added. "Sandra said that she could feel the energy of this man's spirit in and around all the stone walls.

"I asked Sandra what he looked like, and she told me he wouldn't let her see him. She said that he told her, '*She* knows what I look like, why should I show *you?*' He was talking about me."

I was captivated. "He talked with her?" I asked Anna.

"Well, they communicated telepathically," she said.

That made sense. Others who had experienced ghosts in their lives had already told me of telepathic conversations with the spirits.

"So he was talking about you," I pursued. "Had you actually seen him?"

"Yes," Anna told me, "and I really wish that Sandra had been able to see him, too, so I could have had confirmation of what he looked like.

"He woke me up in the middle of the night," she continued matter-of-factly. "We hadn't moved here full time yet, we were still back and forth between Block Island and New York. I was here with Shakespeare, but otherwise I was alone. Shakespeare wasn't here in the room with me." Shakespeare was the Lofaros' brindle pit bull mix dog, a gentle and gentlemanly creature who had died at a ripe old age some months before this interview with Anna.

Anna paused, seeking to clarify her sighting of the ghost. "I can't say that I saw him like a real person, but I had a sense of what he looked like."

That, too, made sense. Some of my ghost seers had a very clearly defined idea of the appearance of their ghosts, others had spoken of a "sense," or a "feeling" of what it was they saw. All who spoke with me knew, positively, that they had seen something out of the ordinary, something supernatural.

"Tell me about him," I said, my hand poised to write.

"He had a long, scruffy, graying beard. An old-fashioned cap, sort of like a baseball cap, only an older style: rounded, with pleats — not close to the head, like a modern cap — and with a bill. It reminded me of an old army hat.

"He had a heavy beige jacket, canvassy looking, with a peplum, and he was wearing a leather belt. He had heavy black boots, and his pants were either stuffed in them, or they were short, like knickers, and baggy. I had a sense of a Revolutionary War uniform, somehow. And he was dirty, as though he'd been out on trails. I thought he might have been a Native American, but the clothes were wrong."

"What did he do?" I asked, impressed by the detailed description.

It shouldn't have surprised me; Anna is a nurse, a gifted seamstress, quilter, and home decorator, and is very detail-oriented.

"Something sat on the foot of my bed, and I woke up and saw him. I knew there was a spirit there — I was frozen in place, and every hair felt as if it was straight up. When he sat on the bed, the bed moved — it went *down* where he sat on it.

"I kept the lights on the rest of the night," she concluded.

"Did he talk to you?" I asked.

"No," she said, "and I was too immobilized to say or do anything."

Anna continued, "The next morning, I had a sense that he was in the bathroom while I was showering. I told him, 'Don't wake me up, don't scare me in the middle of the night. I don't mind if you keep me company during the day, but it's not nice to come into the bathroom while I'm showering.'

"When I was getting ready to leave the house and go back to the mainland, Shakespeare was in the front hall, barking down the hallway. There was nothing there for him to bark at."

Anna backtracked a bit in her narrative. "The time I saw the ghost on the foot of my bed was my second experience with a ghost in the house. The first time was a few years earlier, when we first moved in." Anna confirmed that their home, built by Norris Pike, had been completed in 1990. That was the year they moved in.

"There had been people working in the house. I was downstairs in the kitchen alone, eating lunch. I heard the buzzer go off in the clothes dryer, and at the same time, I heard a vacuum cleaner upstairs."

"I went down the hall, checked the dryer and turned it back on, and when I came back, I could still hear the vacuum cleaner. I wondered who was still up there. I thought everyone who had been working had gone — I looked out the window, and sure enough, all the other cars were gone. Nobody else was in the house.

"So I went upstairs and found the vacuum cleaner in the loft, wide open, with no bag in it, and it was running! I turned it off and it didn't come back on, so it was nothing to do with the wiring or the plug or anything like that. And no person working up there would have turned it on or left it running without a bag in it.

As she took a sip of the warming peppermint-vanilla tea, I asked her if other family members had seen or felt the ghost.

"No, he seems to be around when I'm by myself," she said, "but guests have commented from time to time."

"A couple of years ago, George Marley was staying here with us. In the morning, he asked me, 'Why were you walking up and down all night long?' I told him I hadn't been up at all, I'd been sleeping soundly in bed all night and so had Michael. I told George it must have been the ghost."

George Marley was a young man who, for some time, was the sole choir member at St. Ann's By-the-Sea, leading the congregation in song with his mellow tenor voice. Unfortunately for St. Ann's, he left the Island in 2007 to seek a career on the mainland.

Anna resumed, "Another time, a few years ago, members of the P's and Q's quartet were here for the Block Island Barbershop Concert. The concert was on a Saturday night, and the group had arranged to get up, shower, and work around each other so they could all have a shower before they left in the morning.

"One of the women in the group told me later that she was lying in bed, thinking, 'Do I *have* to get up? I'm so sleepy…' She felt a tap on her shoulder and assumed it was her husband, waking her for her turn in the shower. She heard the shower running. But she looked around, and her husband was fast asleep beside her in the bed. He hadn't been in the shower, and neither had anyone else."

Anna spoke again of the psychic, Sandra, who had visited and felt the presence of the ghost. "Sandra asked me if I wanted the ghost to be gone," Anna said. "I told her, 'No, he's welcome to be here, as long as he doesn't interfere. I don't want him waking me up, or being in the bathroom with me, but if he likes to clean, let him stay! He has to learn to use the vacuum cleaner, though, with a bag in it!'

"I think the ghost and I are at a good place now," she concluded, "I haven't seen him or had any other experiences for awhile, but I've told him I don't mind if he's here.

"Before Sandra left, she told me to bless every outside door and window in the house with holy water, to keep out evil spirits, so I did that."

"But you don't know who it was who might have wanted to buy the land?" I asked her, referring to her protective ghost.

"No, no one seems to know," Anna said, "and it would be farther back than anyone alive would be able to remember.

"I thought he might be attached somehow to the cemeteries — there are two little family cemeteries very near here."

"There are?" Another storyteller had recently posed the theory that cemeteries and moonlight pave the way for ghostly appearances.

Anna told me how to find the cemeteries. "They're on private property, but I think the town maintains them," she concluded.

Mike Lofaro came in from his Tuesday with the Lunch Bunch, a community lunch cooked by volunteers and open to all who wish to partake. There are usually twenty to thirty lunchers in the bunch. Mike is a dedicated dishwasher and kitchen hand every week, and a fine cook when one is needed. We chatted awhile about non-ghostly matters, and I took my leave of Anna and Mike's warm hospitality.

It was an overcast afternoon, but still early enough for good light. As I drove inland, away from the Lofaros' property, I saw two handsome bucks in a clearing near a stone wall. The deer stood like statues, as they often do, staring alertly at my car, unafraid unless I made a move in the wrong direction or a noise that warned of danger. Cemetery sentinels, I decided.

I pulled past the deer, parked at the side of the road and made my way to the top of a knoll. The property was indeed private, but no one was around to answer if I had knocked on a neighboring door and requested permission to be there. As it was, I intended no harm or disturbance to anyone, living or dead.

On the knoll were two family cemeteries, side by side, each in its own little enclosure of stone wall. The Dickens cemetery spanned the decades from 1856 to 1895 and held 17 stones. Eight of them, small and unmarked, were most likely for infants. The Allen plot, dating from 1844 to 1889, contained ten stones, five of them the small, unmarked ones.

I scanned the headstones. Deacon Wanton Allen, who died in 1856 at age 55, had two wives. The first died at 38, and the other outlived the deacon by three decades, dying at age 80. I thought of Mrs. Lofaro's ghost and mused that a deacon probably was not one to pine after property he could not have.

The other two readable headstones in that plot were those of Samuel Allen, possibly a son of Wanton, who lived to age 64; and his wife, Rhoda, who predeceased him by 25 years, dying at age 41. Was the lonely widower, Samuel, the man who had wanted to buy the sheep farm property?

I stepped over the wall to the Dickens cemetery; the plots had no gates or openings. The Honorable Luther Dickens, I noted, died at 56. He, too, had two wives: Mary, who predeceased him by a decade, and Hannah, 23 years younger than Luther, who outlived him by 15 years, dying at age 48. Did the Honorable Luther once want to buy the sheep farm? Another possibility was Raymond Dickens, born in 1802 and living to 83 years of age. His first wife, Isabella, had two children who grew to adulthood; she predeceased Raymond by 35 years. Raymond also survived his second wife, Lucy; just one year young than he, she died two years before him. Raymond's son, Anderson B. Dickens, lived to be 80, surviving his wife, Loxey, by 12 years.

Another family cemetery lies a bit farther away, on private property.

Four adults and four infants are buried there, and the dates of death all fall in the first half of the nineteenth century. Perhaps Mrs. Lofaro's ghost is connected with this plot; it might explain her perception that the ghost had been walking on trails, perhaps through brush, to arrive at her house.

Might any of those so commemorated be the man who wanted to buy a sheep farm, and whose spirit, in recent years, has chosen to make itself visible to only one woman on the property it guards? Who could know?

The steady, cold wind sweeping up through the pastures made the knoll a chill place to linger; I took my leave.

The leisurely drive home that gray midweek afternoon took me through a landscape of incomparable beauty, even (or perhaps especially) at that time of year. Bare trees, the cast of the sky, weathered-shingle houses, stone walls textured with lichen, bayberry thickets punctuated by winterberry — it was harmonious, all of a piece. No other vehicles plied the roads, and only three pedestrians, seeming faceless in their wraps of woolens against the west wind, were to be seen out of doors. The time could have been that day, the day or the week before, or a century or so ago. Whatever time it was, there was no better place to be.

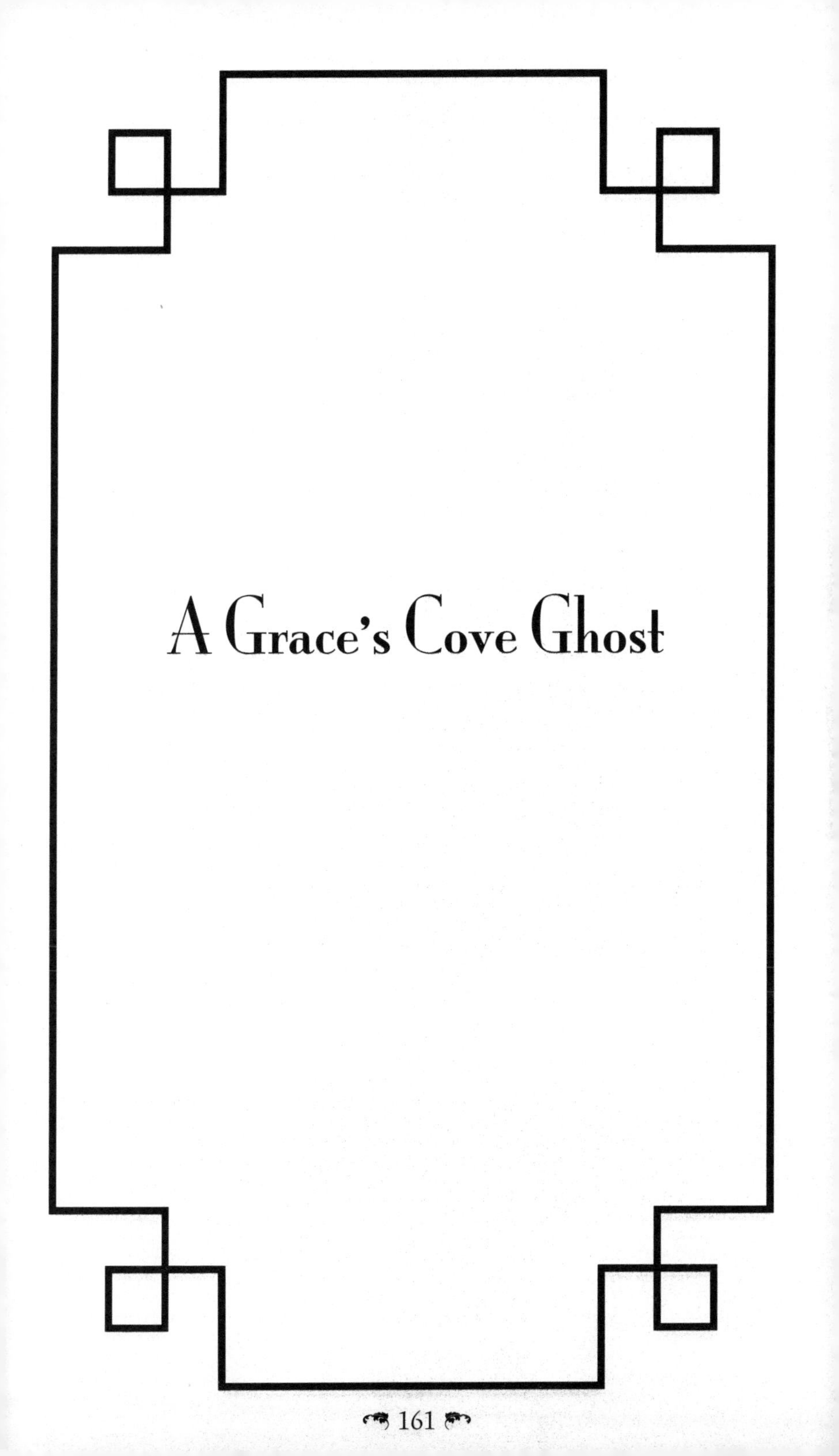

# A Grace's Cove Ghost

"THERE WAS A GHOST IN MY GRANDMOTHER'S HOUSE at Grace's Cove," Howie Rice told me one day as a group of us were having lunch at The Oar. I rummaged for a pen and bit of paper. Howie is a born storyteller and has a mother lode of material, but he's difficult to catch. He is the school bus driver three seasons of the year and a tour bus driver and guide in summer. Or, he's likely as not to be on the road upstate in America, helping Island people get their paperwork through the bureaucratic tangle of the Rhode Island Division of Motor Vehicles. None of these are good places to sit and tell stories over the phone, so it was wonderful to have Howie in captivity long enough to get a story from him.

"It was a Dunn house," he continued. "John or Sam Dunn, I can't remember which. But it was my Grandmother Rice's house, down on Grace's Cove Road. My grandfather used to have cows there in the barn, and chickens."

The house is the Captain John B. Dunn House, built in 1883 by carpenter John Rose. A reference in *Historic and Architectural Resources of Block Island, Rhode Island* describes it as "A 2 1/2-story, 5-bay-façade dwelling with a wraparound front porch, paired brackets on the cornices, and a 1-story ell to one side," and adds helpfully, "Dunn (1841-1916) was a fisherman." The house commands a fine view of Grace's Cove. The barn is still there, though the cows and chickens have long since vanished.

Howie's grandmother's name was Nellie Edna Rice. Behind her former home stands a little red house with a star design on it. I've always liked it, and asked Howie about it.

"The cottage with the star on it came from Branford, Connecticut," he told me. "It was put together here by Fred Steele. Another house, where I used to live, is just over the stone wall from it."

The Rice family once owned 53 acres of land in and around Grace's Cove along Dunn's Cartway, abutting Fiddler's Green and stretching around the Pollitt and Batchelder properties. That part of the Island, in particular, is Dunn territory, though like the other old Island families, the Dunns branched out and had family and properties in many parts of the Island. Bob Pollitt and his nephew, Rick Batchelder, with properties on the Cove, are both Dunn family members, and there used to be many more.

Howie Rice told me that the property known for years as Fiddler's Green once belonged to Archie King, a violin maker — hence the property's name. As a child of nine or ten, Howie used to go down and visit him. "Georgiana King had a house nearby, and I used to go down the road and get jonnycakes from Ada Dunn," Howie recalled.

Getting back to Grandmother Rice's house, he said matter-of-factly, "There was a pump organ in the parlor of my grandmother's house, and at night it used to move."

"You mean you could hear the sounds of moving furniture downstairs during the night?" I asked. I'd heard of furniture-moving ghosts in other places, notably The Nature Conservancy office on High Street, once the home of Gaye Voskamp.

"No," Howie responded. "The house was set up with a living room, parlor, kitchen, front and back bedroom, a hallway, and stairs. My grandmother had the back bedroom, and I had the front one. Almost every night I'd hear the door open, and hear someone either go upstairs, or down the other stairs to the basement.

"The time the organ moved was different. The pump organ moved from one side of the room to the other during the night. We got up in the morning, and it was on the other side of the room, *turned around*, as though it had always been there! There wasn't any noise, and there's *no way* it could have happened — but it did. If the house had shifted, even with an earthquake, the organ couldn't have moved across the room and been turned around like that!

"My grandmother," he added, "was a little tiny woman. She could never have moved it, even if she'd wanted to."

Howie's father, Bob Rice (who preceded Howie, for years, as the Island school bus driver) sold his acreage to Sally Mazzur in 1949 for $5900, and counted himself a fortunate man at the time. The house on Grace's Cove where Bob himself once lived has burned down.

Bob relocated to the corner of Old Town Road and Connecticut Avenue. There he bought a large house once owned by Jennie Barber and formerly run as a boarding house. Bob lived in it the rest of his life, wintering in Brooksville, Florida.

"Something odd happened at that house on Old Town Road, too," Howie remarked as an aside. "One day, Polly, my Dad's second wife, was relaxing and napping on a chair at the back of the house."

Perhaps, I thought, Polly had been out "mowing the back forty," as Bob Rice had often said she was doing, if asked where Polly was when he made his trips to town.

Howie continued, "As Polly sat there, a wedding ring dropped onto her chest. It was a woman's wedding ring, gold. It wasn't hers, and nobody knew where it came from. There was no place for it to drop from. It just appeared." A mystery: and a nice one.

As for the moving pump organ in Grandmother Rice's house, that too is unexplainable. It is tempting to think that some of Archie King's violins were spirited down the road from Fiddler's Green, and Grandmother Rice's parlor rearranged by a ghostly gathering for an evening entertainment of music and dancing. Howie never said anything about hearing music — in fact, he said he and his family heard no noise at all to correspond with the moving pump organ — but ghosts do many things silently, and perhaps they don't need earthly music, audible to human ears, for their spirited dances.

# Franklin Swamp's Elusive Ghosts

"MY BROTHER, BRANDON, HAS A LOT OF GHOST STORIES from when he was building houses on Block Island," Gillian Stevens told me when I called her, out of the blue, in November 2008 and started talking with her about ghosts. Gillian is a sensitive, one who experiences ghosts and supernatural phenomena. I wrote the story she told me and went on my ghostly path as it unfolded, wherever it led me, to write others. When I knew, with a schedule pressing, that I would draft just one more story, signs were pointing to Brandon.

In the summer of 2008, Ann Weinstein had talked to me at one of the summer Arts and Crafts fairs, telling me an anecdote about the building of her house some 30 years ago at Franklin Swamp.

"Thirty years ago, when our house was being built," Ann told me, "the vegetation was sparser around that road going into Franklin Swamp than it is now. You could see a lot from the top of the hill when you turned in.

"I turned in to the road one day, and I could see our house from the top of the road. At the house were three men in coveralls — one was our builder, Brandon Stevens. I got to the house, and the other two men were gone. There was no place for them to go where they wouldn't be seen — they'd just disappeared.

"I've seen fairies that dance on Franklin Swamp," Ann concluded. "*Real* ones!"

I was reminded of the flashes of light energy that Kay McManus and her daughter, Cyndi, reported seeing at their haunted house on Spring Street.

Ann Weinstein told me these things before I knew of Brandon's existence, and months before I learned that he was connected with Gillian Stevens. When Gillian mentioned her brother, Brandon, to me months later, it clicked into place.

And, signs were pointing to Franklin Swamp. After Howie Rice had told me about the ghost at his grandmother's house on Grace's Cove, he added, "There's a ghost at Franklin Swamp. I've heard it's a woman ghost, and there was a tragic death, but I don't know the details and I've never seen her."

As my allotted time to draft material drew to a close at the end of 2008, I picked up the phone and called Brandon Stevens on the west coast of Florida. He of course knew nothing of my existence. I told

him why I had to call him and explained my mission, adding that several people had told me there's a ghost at Franklin Swamp.

"Oh, definitely, there is!" he agreed. "A lot of stuff has happened down there."

I said that Ann Weinstein had told me a story about the building of her house, with the two extra workers who vanished into thin air.

"I don't remember hearing about that! Those other two guys must have been my astral helpers!" Brandon said with a laugh, and continued, "When I built that house for the Weinsteins, I got a call at 5:30 one morning. I answered the phone, and it was Ann's voice at the other end: '*Not* very funny!' she told me. 'We do *not* appreciate your coming into our home in the middle of the night and moving things around!'

"I had no idea what she was talking about, and I was still half asleep! I said, 'Wha-a-a-t?!?' The house had just been finished, and it was the first night Arnold and Ann had spent there.

"Ann told me, 'We got up this morning, and all of our artwork was changed — everything was moved around!'

"It seems Ann and Arnold had just hung all their artwork that day, when they moved into the house," Brandon explained. "During the night, all of it moved or was somehow moved.

"I couldn't help laughing! I told her, 'C'mon, do you really think I came down to your house last night and moved your stuff around? No way! I was tired, I'd been working all day, I was in a bar!'"

Brandon added, "When I was building the Weinstein house, I worked with Kenny Tile, Dave Todd and Nat Gaffett. We were down there late one afternoon in the winter. The winds were picking up and it was getting dark — you know how early it gets dark on the Island in the winter. That day, Kenny and Nat and I were there. We decided to call it a day: 'Yeah, let's go home,' we all agreed.

"As we were leaving, we had the feeling of something watching us. We all felt it. Actually, we had more than just a feeling, but none of us wanted to say anything. But then Kenny said, 'Didn't you see her?'

"We looked at him, and he said, 'The lady in black. Didn't you see her watching us?'

"And then we admitted, yes, we had seen a lady in black, but didn't want to say anything. All three of us saw her."

"What did she look like?" I asked Brandon.

"She was a lady in black, wearing high button boots," he answered. "Her dress was definitely Victorian, a dress with a lot of buttons down the front and a little thin wasp waist. We all concurred in that."

After a moment, Brandon added, "There was a story that a lady down there was killed by her husband in the 1800s. He put an axe in her back."

I shuffled through the rough notes I'd made of Ann Weinstein's conversation with me the previous summer. She had said, referring to a house on a hill north of Franklin Swamp known as West Hill Crest: "At West Hill Crest, in the 1920s I think it was, the daughter of the family who owned the property married a man from off-Island. It was a very unhappy marriage. And then one day, he was found in the shed — a suicide, it was said — and there was an axe in his back. An axe suicide could happen on Block Island.

"I really don't know the details," concluded Ann, "but that's what I was told."

I repeated Ann's story to Brandon. "Oh, I always heard it was the lady in black who was killed by her husband," he said seriously. "That's how the story went."

He added, "I heard that in one house down there, workers doing a renovation took apart the fireplace and found an axe buried in the stonework.

"There's another story about a death at Franklin Swamp," Brandon said. "A kid suffocated in a house there in the 1960s, a teenager. There were a lot of stories at the time; it was mysterious the way he died.

"I heard, second-hand, a story about Alvin Ernst cleaning out the cistern of that house where the teenager died. Alvin had a feeling, working down at that house. This was in the 1960s, in the wintertime — you know, back then nobody would have been anywhere around that time of year. Alvin had the feeling someone was watching him.

"He looked up, and a boulder materialized just above him, a good-sized one. He told someone later that if he hadn't ducked, it would have hit him in the head.

"I was down in that same house with a bunch of guys one afternoon. We wanted to make a beer run. I decided to go, but when I went to the door, I couldn't open it — it wouldn't move! After that, we all tried to open it, and all of us together couldn't get it to move! We tried the other door, it didn't work — and we were all young, strong guys. We tried the windows. None of them would move, or open — we couldn't get out! I decided to break a window so we could get out of the place.

"Just then, Jeff Wagner comes down the hill with a case of beer. He came to the door, opened it, and came right in! The rest of us made a run for the door and Jeff couldn't figure out why there was this mass exodus, all of *us* coming *out*!"

Brandon shared some anecdotes with me of ghosts elsewhere on the Island. "Block Island has a lot of ghosts," he said. "There's a lot of

energy there!

"When we grew up on the Island, Ed Conley was in the high school. He had a Pontiac. One night Ed was driving the Pontiac down the west side, and he felt that someone was watching him. He just couldn't shake the feeling. He knew he was being watched. He looked in the rearview mirror, and he saw two red eyes in there, just staring at him.

"He was telling some of us about it a day or two later; there were skid marks on the road where he'd been driving, where he'd laid on the brakes. He told us that he'd heard a voice in the car — it said, 'Slow down, or you're going to die.'

"Ed said later, that voice was the reason he was still alive. It saved him from having an accident."

Brandon told me about the house he'd built for himself on the Island, "near the airport." I asked him if it was near the one that had burned, that Gillian had told me about, but his was on another side of the airport. "I sold it to Vin McAloon," he told me.

The house is in the vicinity of the Neptune on Connecticut Avenue; Vin McAloon told me it was built in 1974. Vin added that he doesn't believe ghosts inhabit newer houses, and said that he and his family had never experienced any supernatural events there.

Brandon continued, "I was downstairs in that house with Steve Mitchell, and Steve was telling me how to do the kitchen. I heard footsteps upstairs, very distinct ones. I went upstairs and looked, but there was nothing there. I went back downstairs, and I heard the footsteps again, very clearly.

"I went back to the house the next day, and there was a stepladder standing at the top of the stairs. It was standing solid, on four legs — and it tipped over, by itself. There was no movement, no vibration, nothing that would cause it to move. It just went over.

"The doors in that house used to open by themselves sometimes, too. And it wasn't just that the doors opened — the doorknobs would turn, by themselves, and then the doors would open. You could see the knobs turning."

I thanked Brandon for being so forthcoming and helpful about ghosts. He was an entertaining talker and interspersed his talk with a laugh that bespoke a lively memory of his experiences.

Still intrigued by the Franklin Swamp ghost, I called Kenn Fischburg at his home in Connecticut. Kenn and his wife, Kimberly, own an old house at Franklin Swamp, near the water. I asked Kenn about the axe murder, and whether the house involved might be his.

"I've never heard of that one," Kenn replied. "The only death I know about down there was Grace Wheeler's son. He died at her house at Franklin Swamp. Grace couldn't stay in the house after that, so she came and stayed in the house we now have." At the time, Grace owned both houses.

Grace Wheeler: many people I know on the Island, including my husband Rally, knew and had spoken to me, in passing, of Grace Wheeler. When she sold her property at Franklin Swamp, she moved to a house at the bridge on Trim's Pond, on Ocean Avenue. She has grown children with properties on the Island. No one had ever mentioned a son who died — and why would they?

I asked Kenn if he has any ghosts at his house.

"Oh, I don't know," he replied. "The only thing we have is a hot water tank downstairs that goes off by itself. We'll put the switch on, and then we'll find that it's turned itself off and we have to go down and put the switch on again. And there's an emergency light switch down there that goes off by itself, too.

"It's a dirt basement, built in 1898. We've done a lot of work on the house, as you know, but the basement is still the original one."

Kenn concluded, "When the switches go off by themselves, I just smile and say, 'Don't do that again!'"

Early owners of Kenn's house, perhaps the original owners, were Cleon and Sara R. Rose Dunn, who deeded it to Isabelle Littlefield in 1908. Traditional seaweed and peat rights through the waterfront property, referenced in an 1856 deed from Samuel D. Rose to Edward B. Rose, run with the land and are retained by holders of the properties to which those rights were originally accorded.

I still wanted to know more about the axe murder, and the house where the teenager had died. I wanted to know if they had happened at the same house. No one I asked knew about the unhappy marriage that had resulted in a mysterious death by axe. It was all hints and speculation. Yet, three people had heard of a tragic death and a woman ghost, two of the three had differing versions of it, and one of those people had seen an apparition of a lady clothed in black Victorian garb. Did a man murder his wife, or was it he who was found dead? Was the property involved the site of another death at Franklin Swamp, or was it West Hill Crest, off to the north? Or did the woman come from West Hill Crest and move to Franklin Swamp after her marriage?

It was Lew Gaffett, about a week later, who was able to tell me something, at least, of the very sad death of the teenager. "Mark Wheeler died down at Franklin Swamp, at the Josiah Peckham house," he said. "He was working for Payne's Dock when he died. He was found in his upstairs bedroom; he'd died in his sleep. He was an athlete, and he had grown a great deal in the past year."

The words brought home heavy feelings, as the event moved from mystery into hard, recent reality. The death of any child is tragic. I've known of other teenage athletes who have died suddenly, sometimes after a growth spurt that their bodies seemed unable to keep up with. A teenager in the 1960s, Mark Wheeler would have been a contemporary of mine. I felt so very, very sad for his mother, Grace Wheeler.

Grace had acquired the Cleon and Sara Dunn house, where the Fischburgs now live, in July 1959, and it was there that she had gone after losing Mark.

The house she left was a property that she and Ira B. Wheeler had bought for $2500 in February 1959, from the estate of Josiah A. Peckham. Peckham, incidentally, had acquired it in 1938 from Archie King, the violin maker at Fiddler's Green over on Grace's Cove. The Franklin Swamp house, which Lew Gaffett knew as the Josiah Peckham house, is likely the oldest dwelling at Franklin Swamp, built in 1781. The description in *Historic and Architectural Resources of Block Island, Rhode Island* refers to it as the Asa R. Ball House: "A center-chimney cottage with center entrance in the 5-bay façade and an ell to one side. Outbuildings include a barn."

Franklin Swamp, incidentally, is one of a diminishing number of places on Block Island where native cattails are still abundant. In many other Island wetlands, the cattails have been choked out by the invasive grass phragmites.

The two deaths at Franklin Swamp that I was told about in the course of writing this story are serious matter: a violent axe murder, the details lost through the years; and the very sad, relatively recent death of a teenage boy that affected people who are still very much alive.

When people tell me they've heard of a ghost at Franklin Swamp, the response will have to be, "What one? And where?" An axe rumored to have been found sequestered in an old fireplace; a boulder that almost hits a worker in the head; artwork that moves in the night; fairies dancing on the swamp; an astral construction crew; a Victorian lady in black who watches people; a house that won't let people out of it; a nearby house with basement switches that turn themselves off — while the ghost, or ghosts, are mostly elusive, Franklin Swamp seems to have a very large share indeed of Block Island's supernatural energy.

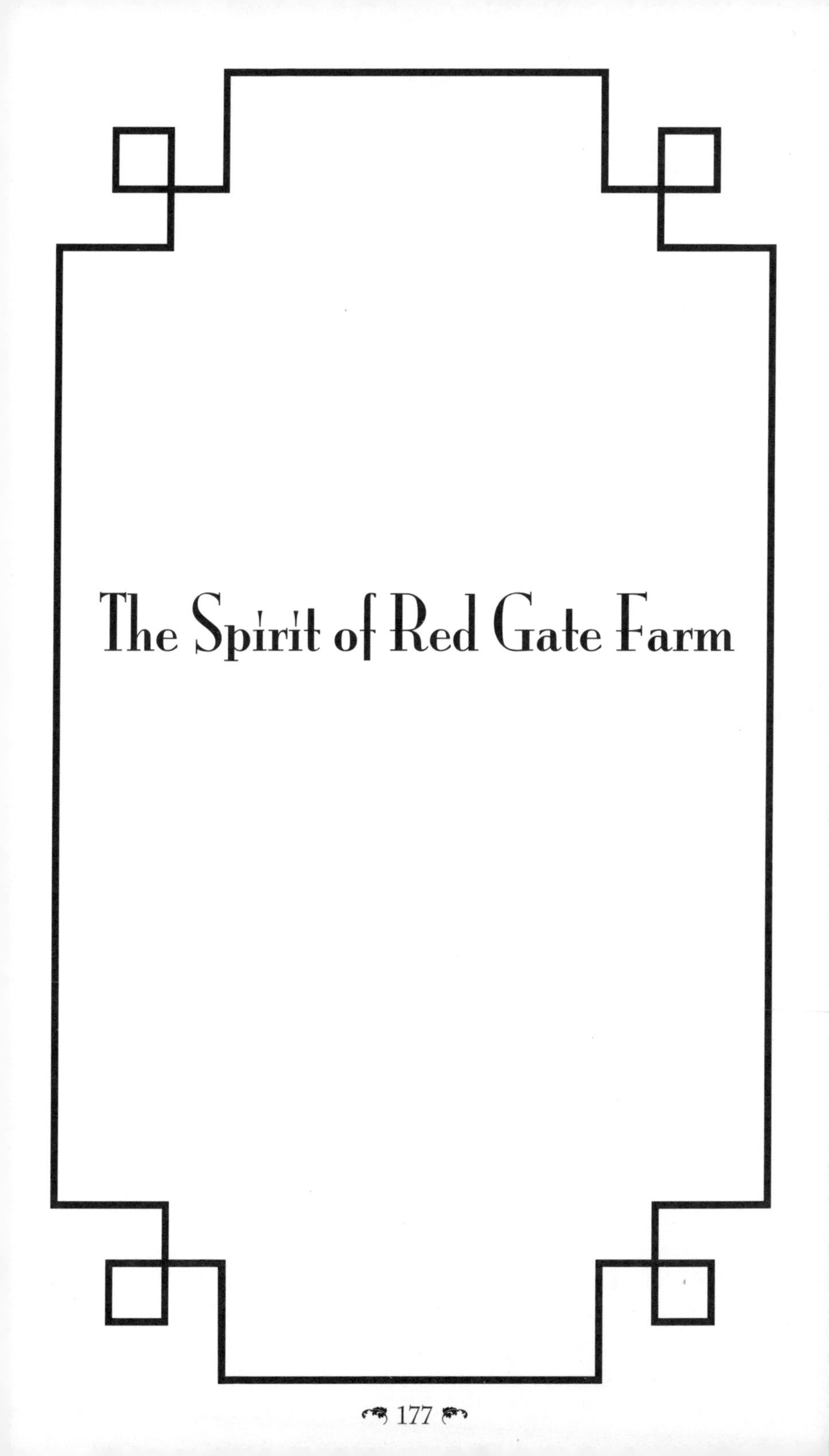

# The Spirit of Red Gate Farm

JUST AS MY LEADS ON BLOCK ISLAND GHOSTS seemed to have dwindled, I received the unexpected gift of a ghost on Christmas Day 2008 from Sandy Gaffett. Sandy and her husband, Lew, brought up five children on Block Island, and all are now living on the Island near their parents. The elder Gaffetts are also proud grandparents to seven grandchildren.

The Gaffett family's main business enterprise was, for years, the Samuel Peckham Inn at New Harbor, now converted to residential condominiums. Many of the units are meant for affordable housing. After "retiring" from ownership of Peckham's, Lew turned his attention to ownership of the friendly neighborhood Albion Pub on Ocean Avenue. Now "retired" once again after selling the Albion, tireless entrepreneur Lew, with that perpetual twinkle in his eye, was mulling over possible new business ventures when Rally and I attended the Gaffetts' Christmas open house at their home in Ebbets Hollow.

Sandy Gaffett, whose full name is Sandra Stokes Madison Gaffett, was for years the director of the Island Free Library, once her children were grown. Sandy's roots go deep on Block Island; her great-grandfather built the large white farmhouse at Red Gate Farm, overlooking New Harbor. The house, across West Side Road from the Block Island Boat Basin, stands adjacent to a cluster of houses known as Trims Ridge. Those houses were built on land that was part of the original Red Gate Farm property. Red Gate Farm is now owned by the Gaffett family's Gate Farm Family Trust.

A year before the writing of this story, the seven-bedroom farmhouse at Red Gate was entirely renovated, with a loving eye to period detail and quality of craftsmanship, by builder Nat Gaffett, Sandy and Lew's son. It is rented out in the summer.

Sandy had told me a couple of years ago that there were probably ghosts at Red Gate Farm. I asked Nat about it once, as he had done so much work on the house. He said he'd never had any supernatural experiences, but recommended that I ask his mother. When I sat with Sandy in her kitchen on Christmas Day, she said, "Oh, I think there are *definitely* ghosts at Red Gate! You hear noises all the time and never know what they are. There's no explanation for them.

"One year, we rented the house to a couple with a baby for the summer. The husband played piano in the bar at Peckham's. He swore there was somebody in the house! He could hear someone talking to him, but not the way a person talks. Sometimes he could understand what was being communicated, but not always.

"He and his wife also said that their baby was particularly happy there, laughing and smiling all the time as if he was being constantly amused. They were surprised that he never cried or seemed cranky; it was as if he always had somebody around looking after him, besides his parents, that he was responding to.

"I think it could have been my grandmother — and from then on, if we heard something in the house that we couldn't explain, we always said, 'Oh, it's Grandma!'"

Sandy pointed to the refrigerator in the corner of her kitchen: "She's right over there," she told me. I looked at the refrigerator, mystified; she left her chair, went over to the corner and plucked a black and white photo in a magnetic frame from the refrigerator door.

"That's Grandma!" she said. "The *Block Island Times* ran a picture of her, asking readers if they knew who this woman was. Her name was Florence Alberta Ball, and she was born on Block Island. She was sent to East Greenwich Academy to finish her education. While she was on the mainland, she met Harold Lester Madison, who was a student at Brown. His family had a large family home in East Greenwich, and Harold was born and brought up there. He went to East Greenwich Academy, too, before he went to Brown.

"When Florence finished at the academy, she came home to Block Island and taught at the Center School until grandpa got through Brown — then they got married."

Florence Alberta Ball was born in 1878, to Captain Martin Van Buren Ball and Mary Jane Hull Champlin Ball. Florence was the second of two children; her older sister, Susan Rebecca, was born four years earlier.

The Center School, where Florence taught, was one of five district schoolhouses that served the Island from 1843, when there were 344 children enrolled in the system, to 1933, when the current, centralized Island school was built in its original form. The Center School served District 2, and the schoolhouse is now a private residence on Center Road. The other four district schools were the Gully School (District 3), now a private home on Payne Road; the Harbor School (District 1), which became the town hall in 1933; the West Side School (District 4), later a parsonage for the West Side Baptist Church and now a private home on West Side Road; and the Neck School (District 5), which no longer exists but once stood across from the large white Hiram Ansel

Ball House, "Cottage Farm," on Corn Neck Road.

In the intervening years, Island demographics have shifted; there are currently about 150 students enrolled in the Block Island School.

Sandy concluded, "Florence was a founding member of the Block Island Historical Society."

Florence and Harold Madison's son, Harold Lester Madison, Jr., married an off-Island girl, Virginia Hollihan. Sandy Gaffett and her brother, Timothy Ball Madison, are their children.

The large white farmhouse at Red Gate Farm, built by Sandy Gaffett's great-grandfather, is known as the Captain Martin Van Buren Ball House. A 2 1/2-story house built with an off-center chimney and a wraparound front porch, it was built from 1892 to 1893 by Island builder Frank Hayes.

Red Gate Farm's owner and builder, Martin Van Buren Ball, lived a long and productive life, from 1839 to 1926. He was involved in farming and mail deliveries to the Island. Captain Ball spent a decade sailing between Newport and Block Island on double-enders, the *Island Belle* and the *Thomas J. Lynch.* He plied the waters for six more years on a schooner, the *Henry B. Anthony*, then spent 21 years as purser on the steamer *George W. Danielson*, of which he was part owner.

During all his years of delivering the post, Captain Ball carried the bag of Island-bound mail on his back through the city of Newport to Commercial Wharf, saw it safely across the water and took it to the Island post office at the other end of the journey.

Said Sandy, of her grandmother Florence, "I always feel her presence in the big house at Red Gate Farm. I get a good, happy feeling when I walk in. I was very close to my grandmother. She taught me lots of things, including how to make doughnuts. I still have her recipe."

Added Ginni Collins, a friend of the Gaffetts who lives at their home at Ebbets Hollow and helps Sandy run the household, "When I went upstairs to the front bedroom of Red Gate Farm, after Nat renovated it, and looked out over the Great Salt Pond, I could feel a presence — it was a warm, loving presence, and I felt as though someone was standing behind me and giving me a big hug."

Sandy told me that Florence was not buried on Block Island, but in the Madison family plot in East Greenwich. In the Island Cemetery, however, a marker in the Martin Van Buren Ball family plot bears Florence's name and date of birth. Perhaps Florence's spirit decided to return and linger here, a place in which she played such a key role. She knew there was an Island resting place for her if she needed it, and perhaps she wanted to see her great grandchildren and great-great grandchildren grow up on the Island where she was born. Her great-grandson's renovation of the farmhouse that her father built must suit her very well as a spirit home.

The spirit of Red Gate Farm was a perfect ghost to hear about from Sandy Gaffett on Christmas Day: Florence Alberta Ball, a beloved grandmother, a teacher, a comforting presence who may talk to people, and who may cause unexpected or unexplainable noises to occur as she moves about her house — but who has the ability to soothe children of all ages, and make them smile.

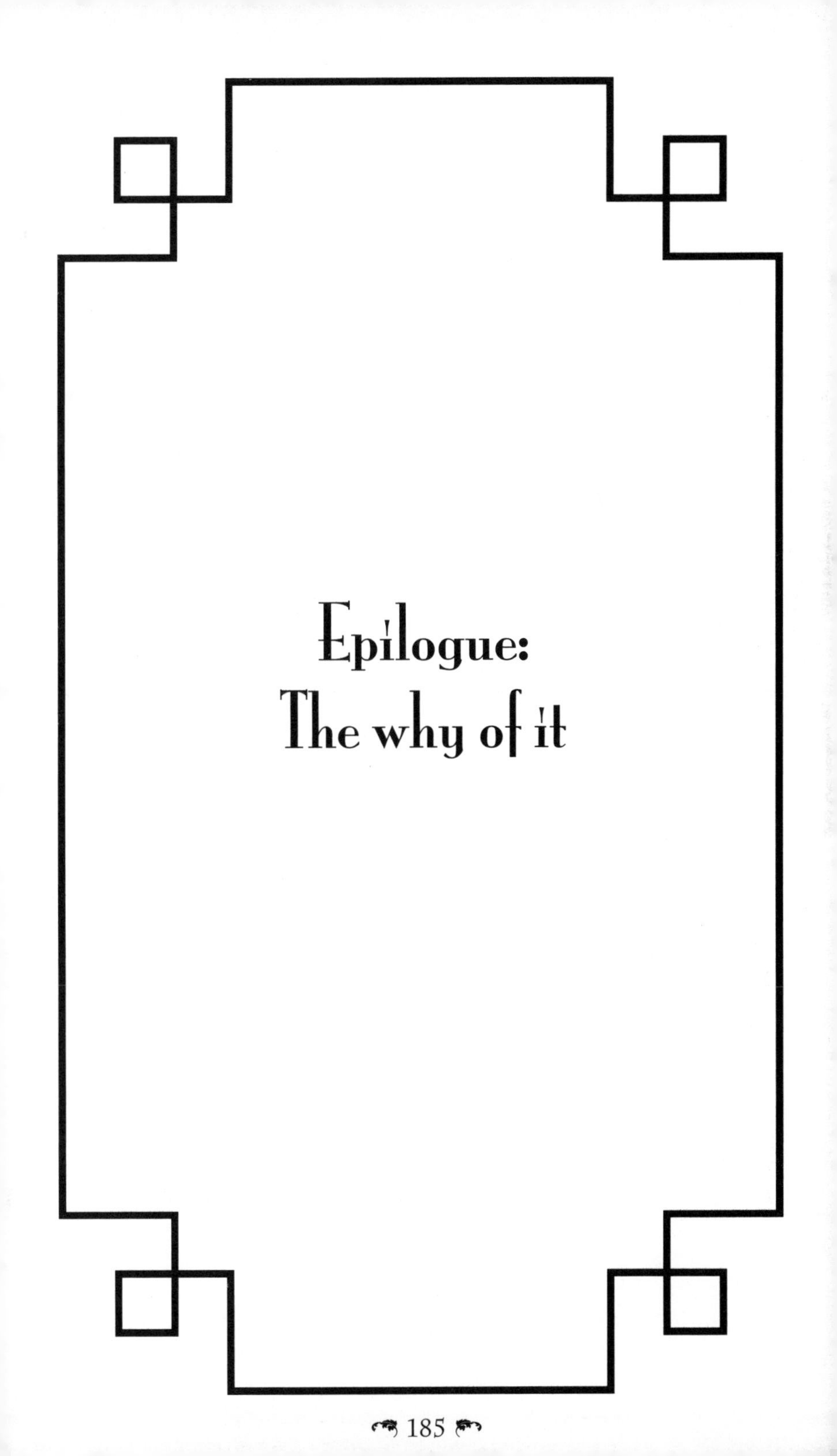

# Epilogue: The why of it

"SO TELL ME, FRAN, how do ghosts fit into your universe here?" asked one of my ghost story tellers, the builder "George," on the dark, damp night in early December when I met him in town to collect his story. "Why do you think they're here?"

"I think ghosts are spirits that have unfinished business in this life," I replied. "I think they're looking for something to complete them and send them on their way, or maybe they're looking after someone here. I've been told that when you see a ghost, you should ask it what it wants."

He nodded thoughtfully. "Do you think spirits go in and out of a ghostly state?" he asked.

I'd never considered that. "I'd always assumed they stayed in a ghostly state, until they're able to move out of it," I replied, "but it would be nice to think they have the option of going in and out of a ghostly existence for some purpose. I've always thought that the choice to be in a ghostly existence is their own choice — though perhaps they're told to enter the world again as ghosts to complete their unfinished purpose."

"Do you think they're unhappy?" George asked.

"Not necessarily," I told him "Some might have been bereaved, and might be back searching this world for the spirits of people they've lost. Some might have left people behind more suddenly than they wanted to, and come back to let the survivors know that they've gone on to another existence, that they're all right, and not completely gone."

I paused and continued, "I think ghosts can be playful, too, and can enjoy 'tweaking' the living a bit, to give them something to think about, just to remind people they're still around. That would be done out of love or affection, and with some sense of humor."

"Do you think it's their preference to inhabit our world?" he wondered.

"I think it might be, for a time, but I don't know if they have the option of staying here indefinitely. Maybe your question as to whether they go in and out of a ghostly state is a key — maybe if conditions are right, or if there's a door between the worlds that suddenly opens, or is found by a human, then ghosts can come through, from one world to the other.

"I do think ghosts are all around us, all the time," I added, "but if there are times or circumstances that cause a door to open, then we become more aware of them. Those are the times when some people are able to perceive ghosts with their senses."

"Do you think a ghost has to want to be perceived to show itself to people? Does the ghost have to want people to be able to experience it with their senses, in order for them to do so?" he asked.

"I used think the ghost has to want to show itself for a person to be able to see it," I replied. "I used to think that's one of the things that makes it a ghost. It's supernatural, after all. But maybe ghosts can be surprised by people who are sensitives, who are quick on the draw at seeing or feeling a ghost. Some ghosts might want to be seen, might want to communicate with the living. Or, if it's a timid ghost, perhaps it would be scared after perceiving that a human has seen it.

"But I don't think people have to 'believe' in ghosts in order to see them. Some people are more sensitive, more receptive, to the supernatural, whether they think they believe in ghosts or not."

People ask me if I believe in ghosts, and my answer is yes, of course: why not? How can one refuse to believe? Listening to people's stories, and knowing that the storytellers are certain, beyond a doubt, that they have seen or experienced something supernatural, catapults me toward belief. Again: why not?

I will leave readers with one more story. I've placed it here in the epilogue because it did not happen on Block Island. It was told to me by a friend, George Blake, who used to live on the Island in the summer, and whom everyone calls Bill. Bill, who turned 82 in December 2008, and his "much younger wife" Marion, had a home on Snake Hole Road for many years. They ran it as a B&B, and called it Bayberry Heath. In the winter, they went to the mainland, where Bill taught at a university. Besides being a teacher, Bill is a gifted poet, short story writer and journalist. He is a person of faith and conscience, an advocate for peace, and his social conscience has driven his politics, his words, and his actions. Beyond all that, he is simply a kind and encouraging person, a positive person to be around. As, of course, is Marion, with her flair for theater and photography, her outgoing personality, and her unerring social sense.

Though they sold their home on the Island's southern bluffs several years ago, Bill and Marion still come to the Island in the summer, rent a house, and stay for a substantial period of time, catching up with friends. In the summer of 2008, as I sat at my table during one of the summer Arts & Crafts Guild fairs, Bill walked over to say hello. Gazing at me very intently, he told me a story.

"When I was five years young," he began, "We lived in Utica, New York. I used to sleep in a little bed in my mother's room, and in the morning she would go downstairs to fix breakfast and call me when it was ready.

"One morning, I woke up to see a young man standing in the doorway of the bedroom. He smiled at me, and waved, but said nothing. Then he disappeared.

"I hurried downstairs, where my mother was making breakfast, and told her what I'd seen. I described the man.

"My mother ran upstairs and returned with a framed photo. 'Look at it carefully,' she said.

"'It's the same person!' I told her.

"Her eyes dropped tears. 'That's a photo of my brother. He was killed in France in the World War. His body was never found.

"'Now eat your breakfast, dear.'

"That's absolutely a true story," Bill concluded.

A short time later, when Bill sent me a book of his poetry, he wrote the same account in a letter that he enclosed in the book.

Why would one not believe in these entities we call "ghosts"?

# Bibliography

*Block Island: The Land*, by Robert M. Downie, Book Nook Press, Block Island, Rhode Island, 1999.

*Block Island: The Sea*, by Robert M. Downie, Book Nook Press, Block Island, Rhode Island, 1998.

*Historic and Architectural Resources of Block Island, Rhode Island*, Rhode Island Historical Preservation Commission, Providence, Rhode Island, 1991.

*Livermore's History of Block Island, Rhode Island*, by Samuel T. Livermore, originally printed 1877, reproduced and enhanced by The Block Island Committee of Republication for the Block Island Tercentenary Aniversary, Block Island, Rhode Island, 1961.

*Old Cemetery at Block Island, R.I.*, copied by Mrs. Helen Winslow Mansfield, 56 Ring Street, Putnam, Connecticut, Dec. 11, 1950.

*Research, Reflection and Recollections of Block Island*, by Frederick J. Benson, Block Island, Rhode Island, June 1961.

Town of New Shoreham land evidence records.

# About the Author and Illustrators:

• **Fran Migliaccio** grew up in Worthington, Ohio, graduated from Wheaton College in Massachusetts, and made her way to Block Island via Boston. A year round resident of the Island for 22 years, she writes for *The Block Island Times* and has written a previous book, *Ghosts of Block Island*. Fran and her husband, Rally, manage the Block Island Boat Basin marina at New Harbor and own a taxi, Mig's Rig. They share their home with Chihuahua doglets Tia Maria and Coco Chanel.

• A year-round resident of Block Island, **Marea Mott** enjoys any photographic challenge, especially those related to haunted spirits. Originally from New York, she graduated from the University of Vermont with a Sociology degree, and later worked with photographers Michael Vaisanen and Annette Berns in Aachen, Germany. She now lives on Block Island, where she and her husband, Peter, are raising their two children.

• **Gillian Stevens** enjoyed the privilege of spending her youth on Block Island. After graduating from the Island school in 1966, she studied at the R.I. School of Design, earning a BFA in Illustration. She went to work briefly as a designer for Hallmark Cards in Kansas City, Missouri, lived in Colombia, South America, for a year, and eventually moved permanently to Saint Petersburg, Florida with her family where she works in her studio as a painter and collage artist. Her artwork is currently shown at the Jessie Edwards Gallery, and her jewelry designs at the Aurora Gallery on Block Island.

• **Susan Filippone** grew up in Warwick, Rhode Island, graduated from Emmanuel College in Boston, Massachusetts with a B.A. in Art. She currently works at *The Block Island Times* as Advertising Design Manager.

• Photographer **Dave Dolan** lives and works on Block Island. He exhibits and sells his work through his online gallery, www.seashorephotography.net.

For information on ordering additional copies of this book, write to:

Fran Migliaccio
P.O. Box 412
Block Island, RI 02807

or visit website www.blockislandghosts.com

# The Reader's Own List of Ghost Rules and Ghost Etiquette

Do you know, or have you thought of, any new or different bits of ghost lore, ghost rules, or ghost etiquette?
Here is a blank writing space for you to make your own list: